INSTITUTIONAL THEORY
OF MONEY

THE ESSENCE AND LEGAL STATUS
OF MONEY AND SECURITIES

A. YU. GRIBOV

ACADEMUS
Publishing

Academus Publishing
2015

Academus Publishing, Inc.

1999 S, Bascom Avenue, Suite 700 Campbell CA 95008
Website: www.academuspublishing.com
E-mail: info@academuspublishing.com

The right of A. Yu. Gribov is identified as author of this work.

Translated and copyedited by ELSE Professional Business Editors, Moscow
Literary Editors, Translators: Daria Kulesh, Emma Fenwick

ISBN 10: 1 4946 0000 5
ISBN 13: 978 1 4946 0000 6
DOI 10.12737/6433

Introduction

The aim of this study is to deduct and demonstrate current definitions (which are essential for the normal functioning of a country's
financial system) of a security, money, currency and, most importantly, of the rules of circulation for different forms of money and
securities.

Definition of a security

A *security* is a document that has been completed in the prescribed
manner and in accordance with compulsory requirements, and which
secures a sum total of property rights and non-property rights that are
subject to certification, concession and unconditional realisation as
prescribed by federal law, and which may be alienated by the right-
possessing side to any party, regardless of the wishes of the legally bound
side.

In some cases, for example, with acceptance of a promissory note,
the legally bound side can change without the agreement of the right-
possessing side.

With the alienation of a security, all rights (obligations) secured by
it transfer in the aggregate.

A security has an obligatory nature regardless of which bearer it is
filled in for.

A security of which the owner's rights are secured in a special register (ordinary or computerised) is a *registered security*.

In a case provided for by law or in accordance with it, for the realisation or alienation of rights certified by a security, evidence of these
rights, which is kept in a special register, is sufficient.

A security for which the right-possessing side is the owner of its
bearer is called a *bearer security*. A bearer security is completed in a
single copy.

Rules for circulation of securities

Securities, with the exception of bearer securities, are treated in
accordance with liability laws.

Bearer securities are treated in accordance with laws of estate, but
they are issued and redeemed in accordance with liability laws.

Definition of money

Various property goods can be used as money — objects, liabilities and entity-liability combinations, which fulfil the following functions of money:

- a measure of value;
- means of circulation;
- means of accumulation.

Money can have value:

1) either on the strength of its natural useful properties — use value (commodity money):
- precious and other metals;
- rare minerals;
- hides, grain, livestock;

2) or as containing a liability (credit money or financial money):
- promissory notes;
- banknotes and billon coins containing an insignificant amount of a precious metal;
- deeds for accounts in banks and registers;
- bonds;
- cheques;
- other securities;

3) or as entity-liability combinations, for example, coins with a specifically valuable content of a precious metal[1].

Definition of currency

Currency — liabilities, stipulated for circulation, of a State bank (treasury, reserve system) — State cash or non-cash money — is defined as bearer securities issued by the State without a time-limit for presentation in the bearer's name with an endorsement, which must be accepted in all regions of a country in accordance with the norms of its public law.

---

[1] Extremely rarely encountered in practice. The circulation of money as entity-liability combinations with components that are comparable in significance is not included in this study.

Rules for circulation of different forms of money

The rules of circulation of different forms of money are defined by the rules of circulation for those material goods that fulfil the functions of money.

According to the circulation rules, all forms of money can be divided into three broad categories: entities, liabilities and derivative securities (derivatives).

Entities:

1) natural, non-standardised commodity money;

2) metal ingots of exact weight;

3) full-weight metal coins.

This type of money (entities) is treated in accordance with the rules applied in the law of estate/proprietary law.

Pure liabilities:

1) registered securities in cash form:

a) registered bills;

b) registered bonds, promissory notes of banks, and other quasi-money;

c) nominal shares and other stock valuables;

2) nominal accounts in non-cash form:

a) non-cash currency (deposit money, cheque accounts);

b) any business-type accounts, which reflect:

• promissory notes;

• bonds, banks bills, and other quasi-money;

• nominal shares and other stock valuables.

This type of money (liabilities) is circulated in accordance with the rules applied in law of obligations.

Derivative securities, where the right to own an entity, which is the bearer of the liability, generates a legal binding relationship with the debtor:

1) ordinary bearer bills;

2) banknotes from private banks;

3) cash currency — State bank notes and coins;

4) bonds, bank bills, and other quasi-money in the form of bearer securities;

5) shares and other stock valuables in the form of bearer securities.

Such derivative securities are circulated in accordance with laws of estate, with the exception of their issue and redemption, in which case they are circulated in accordance with laws of obligation.

In this study, use has been made of detailed quotes from Russian and foreign researchers into the legal and economic nature of money, in order to deduct and demonstrate these definitions and rules.

Part I
WHY IS AN INSTITUTIONAL THEORY OF MONEY NEEDED?

On errors in the legal treatment of the concept of money and securities and their consequences

In 1995, during Russia's first banking crisis, the largest of the ruined banks was the Moscow interregional commercial bank (MMKB) — formerly Promstroibank of the Moscow region. Despite the considerable sum of its assets, the bank returned very little in the way of funds to the creditors. The bank's lawyers played a large role in this, taking an extremely interesting stance, which contradicted the economic treatment of the category «money».

Relying on the Civil Code of the Russian Federation (CC RF), which had been adopted a year before the crisis, they maintained that money is not a liability, but an entity. And since the money which remained in the assets of the bank was the money of investors — natural persons, then the creditors — legal persons — could not demand from the bank entities that did not belong to them.

There was some legal logic in this, and it led to certain results. If the clients of the bank — legal persons — could claim from a legal point of view that their monetary relations with the bank were subject to liability laws, and not laws of estate, then they would have succeeded in recovering much more from the ruined bank.

The described legal risk of keeping and using money through a bank system is becoming extremely high, which leads, throughout the Russian economy, to a reduction in the amount of non-cash monetary circulation in the country, and, consequently, to a fall in gross domestic product (GDP).

Thus it is vitally important to take away this legal risk, not only for the benefit of the banking sector, but also in order for Russia's economy as a whole to develop normally.

Having begun to take shape, the practice of market relations has nevertheless defined non-cash money as a liability of a bank, for current accounts and for thrift accounts, respectively.

But in relation to paper money, the country's leading legal experts did not waver. Paper money is a physically tangible entity, as they said and wrote in Article 128 of the Civil Code of the Russian Federation (Art. 128, CC RF): «Entities, **including money and securities,** are objects of civil rights...»

The ambivalence of the economic nature of money and its legal definition

> *Natural law is the law established among people by natural reason.*
>
> Institutes of Gaius

The development of economic market relations exposes the contradictions that have accumulated between practice and theory, both in economics and in interdependent legislation.

The country's leading economists pay too little attention to the drawing up and expert examination of economic legislation that already exists and that is being developed, which regulates, in particular, turnover of funds and financial turnover, which leads to a disparity of leading legal treatment of money and securities to their economic content, which must determine their legal formulation. The rules incorrectly defined by legislation for the circulation of money and securities have a negative influence both on turnover/circulation of monetary funds in the country and monetary policy as a whole.

These kinds of relations are known as ambivalent, because, in a material sense, developing social relations are the origins of law, and these relations are linked to the method of producing material goods, the material conditions of the life of society, the system of economic ties, forms of ownership as the ultimate cause of origin and actions of law.

Are we able to accept the provisions of Article 128 of the CC RF, knowing that they do not correspond with basic economic principles?

Cicero affirmed that, «true law is a reasonable tenet that corresponds with nature»; «natural law came about earlier than any written law»; «law is established by nature, and not by human decisions and decrees»; **«a law established by people may not violate order in nature»; «the con-**

formity or disparity of human laws with nature (and with natural law) appears as the criterion and standard of their justice and injustice»[1].

Karl Marx later concluded that law and the State relate to super-structure with regard to basic industrial and economic relations. Legal relations arise from economic relations, serve them, are a necessary form of their expression and existence.

Since the economy is the basis of a State, and the State and law are its superstructure, if we continue the analogy, we must come to the conclusion that theory must be the foundation of legislation.

Basis	Economy	Political economy
Superstructure	Law and State	Legislation

In one of his letters to C. Schmidt, F. Engels explained: «...the effect of State power on economic development can be threefold. It can work in the same direction — then development is made more quickly; it can work against economic development — in which case, now, for every large people it crashes over a certain period of time; or it can create obstacles to economic development in certain directions and push it in other directions. This case eventually leads back to one of the first two. However, it is clear that in the second and third cases political power can cause the greatest harm to economic development and can waste an enormous amount of effort and material»[2].

Legislation that contradicts its foundation — economic theory — is an obstacle to the development of a country's economy.

---

[1] A History of Political and Legal Studies / edited by V. S. Nersesyants. Moscow, 1998. pp. 84–86 (История политических и правовых учений / Под ред. В.С. Нерсесянца. М., 1998. С. 84–86).

[2] *K. Marx, F. Engels.* Complete works. 2nd edition. Vol. 37, p. 417 (*Маркс К., Энгельс Ф.* Соч. 2-е изд. Т. 37. С. 417).

Methodological foundations of analysis: theories of money and the institutional approach

The problem of money has been considered by many schools of economics, but, unfortunately, it occupies little space in institutionalist theory. Institutionalists most commonly examine property rights, transaction expenses, the essence of companies and the role of the State in the market economy. The problem of money is usually posed only from the point of view of defining money supply and demand for money.

The provisions of neo–institutionalism, and especially the economics of law, which allowed interrelationships between economics and legislation to be revealed, became the methodological basis of analysis.

I.P. Nikolaeva[1]

Theories of money

Russian examiners of questions concerning the evolution of the essence and forms of money traditionally take the classic approach, on the whole understanding money to mean a particular type of goods. This approach dates back to the Marxist tradition, although these days it is experiencing significant modifications.

Researchers in other countries treat money on the basis of a whole range of theories, which should be categorised as follows:

1) on the influence of money supply on the economy:
- the quantitative theory of money;
- I. Fisher's quantitative theory of money;
- the Cambridge version of the quantitative theory of money;
- modern/contemporary monetarism;

2) the functional theory of money;

3) the theory of the proper essence of money:
- commodity;
- metallic;
- nominalist;
- State, etc.

---

[1] Comment of the official opponent on A. Yu. Gribov's dissertation on the subject of «The institutional nature of modern money and securities».

The aforementioned theories explore those aspects of money and money handling which are not examined in this study. Thus, the metallic theory of money (T. Men, D. North, A. Montchrestien, K. Knies) regard valuable metal money as the wealth of a nation. The quantitative theory of money (C. Montesquieu, D. Hume, J. M. Keynes, I. Fisher, M. Friedman et al.) dwells principally on the direct relationship between the growth of money supply in circulation and a rise in commodity prices. The informational theory of money regards money as information[1].

As the main challenge of this study is the complex theoretical analysis of the nature of contemporary money and securities as a category of economics, in order to show the contradictions between how they are treated economically and legislatively, a particular methodological approach is proposed.

The fact is that, on the one hand, money is an objective phenomenon originating and developing as a result of the natural evolution of commodity production, and on the other hand, its real forms are strengthened by legislation, which is a prerogative of the State. Money circulation and movement of securities is also regulated by the State.

In this study, an attempt is made to move away from the traditional approach, as not one of the theories listed above can, on its own, serve as a methodological foundation of analysis.

The first most important methodological principle is the **pluralistic conceptual approach**, in accordance with which principles and tools of exploration of several economic theories are used: the commodity, nominalist, State and functional theories of money, as well as a number of neo-institutional ideas.

In the commodity theory, money is regarded as a special kind of universal commodity, which is used as a universal equivalent, and through which the value of all other goods is reflected. Money is a commodity which performs a range of functions, and is, figuratively speaking, «the good of all goods»[2].

---

[1] For more details see Dictionary and guide to contemporary money and monetary institutes, by V. Yarovitskii. http://www.yur.ru/money/sprav/1.html (*Яровицкий В.* Словарь-справочник по современным деньгам и денежным институтам // http://www.yur.ru/money/sprav/1.html)

[2] B. A. Reisberg, L. S. Lozovskii, E. B. Starodubtseva. Modern Economic Dictionary. (*Райзберг Б.А., Лозовский Л.Ш., Стародубцева Е.Б.* Современный экономический словарь // http://www.smartcat.ru/Terms/term_10234006.shtml)

However, this is insufficient for a description of money, particularly its modern forms. It is impossible, using only the tools of the commodity theory of money, to discover the essence of financial money, such as shares and other stock. Furthermore, the essence of a phenomenon can never express the total wealth of its actual content and forms of manifestation. Therefore, our research is also based on the neo-institutional theory.

Neo–institutional theory and economic analysis of law

Unlike other economic theories, the neo-institutional theory analyses **economic categories as a result of the concerted actions of individuals**. Economic categories such as money, goods and the market are, from the perspective of this theory, the coordinated result of interaction between individuals, consciously making specific concessions for each other in order to achieve a goal and realising individual interests, which could otherwise never be achieved.

It should be noted that economic theory, with the development of different branches of neo-institutionalism, encompasses all the new spheres of analysis — from legal matters to problems in making objective and democratic choices. «Economic imperialism» has even begun to make accusations against it. Neo-institutional theory, which is made up of multiple trends, does not contradict other trends in economic theory, but, rather, fills their gaps.

As a methodological foundation for research, a new branch of neo-institutional theory is applied in this study — **economic analysis of law**, which was identified as an independent discipline in the mid 1960s. R. Coase and R. Posner became key figures in the development of economic analysis of law.

The works of G. Becker also had enormous significance for the economic analysis of extra-market forms of conduct, criminality in particular.

Economic analysis of law conducts analysis using economic methods, but its fields of investigation include both the economy and the legal sphere.

In Russia's study of economics, the principles of economic analysis of law are only just being applied, while in other countries, particularly the USA, it has already become a powerful trend. Economic analysis of law, which emerged in the 1970s, is now one of the most influential trends in the study of the economy of the USA and other western countries. There probably remains not one legal standard, nor one single element of a legal system that has not been subjected to economic analysis of law in recent times. In practice, this is conveyed in the successive transfer of micro-economic analytical instruments to non-market relations, one of which is law.

A classic work in the field of economic analysis of law is the book by Richard Posner, «Economic analysis of law», published for the first time on the USA in 1972. It was not translated into Russian and published in Russia until 2005[1]. Economists of this type have made a contribution by proving that the legal system and matters of its function have clear explanations within the framework of economic theory.

Economic analysis of law studies two types of problems: firstly, how economic agents react to various legal establishments; and secondly, how legal standards themselves change under the influence of economic factors.

It is worth noting that our analysis of the interaction between the economic and legal natures of money takes place in the course of economic analysis of law, and so the mutual influence of the economic nature of money and law will be examined.

The basic thesis of economic analysis of law consists in the following: legal rules must imitate the market. According to American economist J. Hirshleifer, the conceptual framework of economic analysis of law comprises three theorems: the theorem of A. Smith, the theorem of R. Coase and the theorem of R. Posner[2].

---

[1] *R. Posner.* Economic analysis of law: 2 vol. set, M., 2005. (*Познер Р.* Экономический анализ права: В 2 т. М., 2005) (*N.B.*: R. Posner is not an economist, but a judge.)

[2] *J. Hirshleifer.* Evolutionary models in economics and law: cooperation versus conflict strategies // Research in Law and Economics, 1982. Vol. 4. P. 2–4 (quote from R.I. Kapelyushnikov. Economic theory of property law (methodology, basic concepts, circle of problems). Moscow, 1991 (*Капелюшников Р.И.* Экономическая теория прав собственности (методология, основные понятия, круг проблем). М., 1991). // http://lib.web-malina.com/getbook.php?bid=2197&page=10

We shall examine the essence of these theorems, as well as the possibility of adapting them to our own study.

According to **A. Smith's theorem**, voluntary exchange increases the welfare of participants in a transaction. From this he concludes that legislation must, as far as possible, encourage exchange, firstly, removing artificial barriers of any kind, and secondly, ensuring legal protection of voluntarily concluded agreements. Correspondingly, legislation must ensure the safety of participants in contracts, that is, the investors and the owners of securities, etc.

According to **R. Coase's theorem**, all opportunities for a mutually profitable exchange are fully concluded by the interested parties themselves, on the condition that transaction expenses are nil, and the property rights precisely defined. Consequently, legislation must ensure clear specification of property rights for all economic resources, such as money and securities.

R. Posner's theorem is linked with R. Coase's theorem. It states that when transaction expenses are positive, that is, when in the course of the exchange objective obstacles arise, which prevent the achievement of effective results, different variants of the distribution of property rights prove not to be of equal value from the point of view of the interests of the company. As a result, legislation must elect and establish the most efficient distribution of property rights of all available options.

Analysis of law according to R. Posner

Posner deducted a **criterion of efficiency of legal decisions**. In his opinion, **legal decisions must correspond with the criterion of economic efficiency.** He defines this criterion either as the «principle of maximisation of wealth» or as the «principle of minimisation of transaction costs». It is necessary to reform legal institutions only on the basis of considerations of efficiency.

In the theory of economic analysis of law, the legal system begins to reflect the market, and is regarded as a mechanism that regulates the distribution of limited resources. **A legal system must imitate the market.** Therefore, legal standards, like elements of the market, must be established on the basis of considerations of efficiency.

The following general requirements for a legal system result from such an approach.

1. The law must facilitate a reduction in transaction costs, in particular, eliminating artificial barriers in the course of a voluntary exchange, and ensuring the execution of concluded contracts.

2. The law must also clearly define and reliably protect property rights, thus impeding the transformation of voluntary transactions into compulsory ones. The elimination of uncertainties in allotment of property rights will lead to expansion of the field of voluntary exchange.

3. Legislation must elect and establish the most efficient possible distribution of property rights, similar to what economic agents would reach themselves, if not hindered by high transaction costs[1].

The normative conclusions of economic analysis of law have already begun to penetrate the judicial and legislative practice of many countries. Posner's thesis on the «imitation» of the judicial system helps the market to reveal and get rid of norms that prevent the economy from working efficiently[2]. Leaning on Posner's thesis, we shall compare the economic and legislative interpretation of money and securities, in order to expose the basic trends of overcoming inconsistencies between them and thus to construct legal standards based on the criterion of economic efficiency.

The selection of methods of legal protection of property rights must also be directed by the criterion of economic efficiency. Posner sees a legal analogy of the market in the case-law system. Within the framework of this system, he claims, decisions are made by courts in general in accordance with the criterion of economic efficiency[3]. In the general mass of publications on the economic analysis of law, in concrete examples of different precedents and legal standards, it is argued that these precedents and standards were actually established in conformity with the principles of economic efficiency.

As the economic analysis of law draws heavily on the neo-institutional **theory of property rights**, which was developed in the second half

---

[1] See: *N.V. Yartseva*, Modern Concepts of an Economic Idea: textbook (*Ярцева Н.В.* Современные концепции экономической мысли: Учеб. пособие) // http://irbis.asu.ru/mmc/econ/u_sovrcon/4.4.5.ru.shtml

[2] Ibidem.

[3] See: *R. A. Posner*. Economic analysis of law. Boston, 1972. P. 102.

of the XXth century by American economists and winners of the Nobel Prize in Economics in 1991, R. Coase and A. Alchian, we shall dwell on a few aspects necessary for our analysis. (American economists Y. Barzel, H. Demsetz and R. Posner, amongst others, later actively participated in the development and use of this theory.[1])

The fundamental challenge posed by the theory of property rights, as formulated by these western economists, consists in the analysis of the **interaction between the economic and legal systems**. Property rights determine which costs and remunerations agents can expect for their actions. Restructuring property rights leads to changes in the system of economic incentives, and the altered behaviour of economic agents will be a reaction to these changes. This logic — from the structure of rights through the incentives system to the behavioural consequences — is clearly reflected in the analysis of the processes of specification or dilution of property rights.

The concept of property rights in the context of a new approach extends to all rare goods. **It encompasses powers over both material objects and human rights.**

Let's single out the most important factor of this definition for us: the theory of property rights uses the term «property rights», not «property». Property is not a resource in itself, but property is formed by a share of rights to use a resource.

Historical school of law

As economic ideas began to move into the field of law, legal ideas began to move into the area of economics. At the onset of the nineteenth century, a new, so-called historical school of law was formed, which opened the way to a different understanding of law. According to this school, **law is a product of life**, which reflects only those relations that are formed in reality.

The law changes whenever culture, national consciousness and a way of life move forward. Through this point of view it is possible to explain the meaning and essence of known problems, in order to be

---

[1] For more details see: «Terminology of contemporary market economics» (Термины современной рыночной экономики) // http://sre.mnogosmenka.ru/sre0721/sre0727. htm

aware of the real needs of active life, which must be regulated by them (it is not clear what must be regulated and how). **The dependence of law on the economy is particularly manifested in the realm of civil law.** Like law, which regulates relations between parties as regards the ownership of property, it is particularly intertwined with various factual peculiarities, which characterise economic life of this people in this day and age.

For example, the more industry and trade are developed, the more immovable property rights come into line with movable property rights, and freedom of circulation, which characterises movable property, gradually applies to immovable property as well. In the developed industrial and commercial way of life, various constraints are more and more commonly/frequently revoked.

For a clear understanding of the legal system of society, apart from studying resolutions of positive law, attention must be paid to actual economic relations, which result in legal standards. Therefore, in order to understand economic relations in a certain country, one must familiarise oneself with the basic institution of law. Legal standards in relation to property and contracts are particularly important here. The level of freedom of individuals, the boundaries and content of property rights, conditions of concluding contracts — such are the main categories of legal standards on which the system of the commercial economy depends.

The inadequate economic competence of many leading Russian legal experts and legislators, both in matters of fundamental political economic theory and in the use of terms, has caused, first and foremost, a woolliness of economic definitions in existing legal field in Russia and a lack of economic expert examination of laws.

Evolutionary institutionalism

The evolutionary branch of institutionalism[1], whose founder, Douglas North, became a Nobel Prize winner at the end of the 1970s, also provides, in our opinion, the necessary theoretical basis for the analy-

---

[1] Evolutionary institutionalism became firmly established as a particular trend in 1982, when 'An Evolutionary Theory of Economic Change' by R. Nelson and S. Winter was published. The book was published in Russian in 2000. Evolutionary changes in economic literature in Russia and elsewhere are thoroughly examined: J. Shumpeter,

sis of changes in legislation, concerning the treatment of modern money and securities, which can be viewed as a particular case of the institution.

From the point of view of North and his followers, the evolution (history) of the economy of different countries must be discussed from the perspective of institutional changes. Institutions are the «rules of the game» in any society, a restrictive framework which limits interrelations between people, reduces the uncertainty of these interrelations, and brings order to everyday life. «Institutes,» writes North, «create basic structures, with the help of which people throughout history have achieved order and thus lowered the level of their uncertainty»[1].

According to North, the institutional environment evolves over time. Institutional changes can occur spontaneously (then the informal rules of the game change for separate economic subjects), and deliberately, under the influence of the State, changing certain rules of the game[2].

Russia's market economy is coming into being, that is, institutional changes are taking place. Moreover, they are not the result of previous courses of development, i.e. the changes are revolutionary. In the meantime **transformation costs** are springing up.

V. M. Polterovich notes that the most important factor of transformation expenses is **disorganisation**[3]. There are two aspects of this to distinguish.

Firstly, in the process of reform, **the old system is destroyed before the efficiency of the new one becomes apparent.** The manifestation of this phenomenon of disorganisation represents the inadequacy of the legislative treatment of money and securities in relation to their modern economic nature. Market agents are settling in the private sector that is being generated in anticipation of future revenue; however, only some of them realise their expectations, since they can suffer losses as a result

---

R. Nelson and S. Winter, W. Rostow, M. Todaro, W. Lewis, R. Nureyev, V. Mau, A. Illarionov, S. Bessonov, D. North, R. Hardin, B. Weingast, P. Milgrom.

[1] *D. North.* Institutes, institutional changes and functioning of the economy. Moscow, Nachala, 1997. P. 32.

[2] For example, formal rules of the game borrowed from outside Russia do not correspond with customs and traditions accepted in Russian society, and such borrowing cannot be successful. Economic development is slowing down due to the predominance of local informal rules.

[3] *V. M. Polterovich.* On the road to a new theory of reform (*Полтерович В.М.* На пути к новой теории реформ) // http://ecsocman.edu.ru/ecr/msg/182837.html

of the inadequacy of legislation in relation to the nature of modern money and securities.

Secondly, there is a **lack of coordination in the actions of different agents, including the State, which does not provide market agents with an efficient legal system in accordance with the criterion of imitation of the market in law.**

Inefficient stable standards of conduct are known as institutional traps. These include barter, non-payments, insufficient guarantee on deposits, and so on. V. M. Polterovich notes: «Countries with a developed market economy have different systems of market institutions. Each of these has taken shape under the influence of the culture and history of that particular country. With borrowing comes the danger that **institutional conflict** may arise between standards that have taken root and those that are being instilled. Sometimes institutional conflict leads to the appearance of non-viable institutions — such as the law on bankruptcy during a non-payment crisis. However, in many cases, stable yet ineffective formations appear — these are **mutants**, which are a type of institutional trap»[1]. In Polterovich's opinion, «what is needed is not a 'strong' but an 'efficient' government. Efficiency means the development and maintenance of mechanisms to expose and integrate public preferences, orientation towards goals shared by society, and the ability to achieve them»[2].

Economic agents have the right to request the State to create an efficient legal system. This position is substantiated within the framework of the property rights theory, which was proposed by D. North. A State can be seen as an agency that provides services in exchange for taxes: «...we pay the government in order that it establish and protect property rights»[3]. The creation of a legal system to protect property rights requires the delegation of powers from the central authorities to its agents. But the agents, naturally, will be opportunistic. Consequently, the structure and conduct of bureaucracy (executors of the wishes of the management) will be determined by transaction costs to control it.

---

[1] Ibidem.
[2] Ibidem.
[3] See: *R. I. Kapelyushnikov*. Economic theory of property rights (methodology, basic concepts, circle of problems). Moscow, 1991. // http://lib.web-malina.com/getbook. php?bid=2197&page=10

Our study of the essence and forms of money is also based on the methodological **historical method principle**. According to this principle, the concept of «money» as a scientific category is examined in historical development. Money only arises when market relations appear, and evolves along with these relations. The development of this category brought about the need to study it and, correspondingly, the appearance of different scientific approaches.

As the **methodological premise** of our analysis, differentiation, on the one hand, and the similarity between the concepts of «money» and «securities» on the other, are used. This makes it possible to develop unified principles of their legislative regulation.

In uncovering the economic essence of money, we shall adhere to the following **methodological principles:**

- the study of the essence of money presupposes the exposure of its internal characteristics;
- analysis of the essence of money must begin with its origin, i.e. with defining the reasons and prerequisites of its appearance;
- the question of the essence of money must be examined in relation to all transactions involving money.

The theoretical arguments listed contain general tenets concerning the methodology of the study of the economic and legal aspects of money and securities. It is necessary to add methodological approaches to concrete theoretical problems, and this will be done in the following discourse.

Legal differences in the treatment of objects and liabilities

> *An object has its own distinguishing signs, the most important of which is the externally expressed material form of an object.*
>
> D. V. Murzin[1]

There is a clear difference between property laws and liability laws. The application of either standard is mutually exclusive.

---

[1] *D.V. Murzin*. Securities — incorporeal goods. Legal problems with the contemporary theory of securities. Moscow, 1998. P. 16 (*Мурзин Д.В.* Ценные бумаги — бестелесные вещи. Правовые проблемы современной теории ценных бумаг. М., 1998. С. 16).

When jus ad rem grants its bearer the opportunity to directly exert influence upon it (when the object of the law is the article), the law is called *proprietary*. In Rome, property law was closely related to proprietary interest, and ownership and other laws on other people's articles are closely linked to them. In cases where the subject has no direct right to an article, but has only the right to demand that another party gives him an article, this law is called *contractual*. Thus, differences between proprietary and contractual laws develop according to the object of the law: **if the object of a law is an article, then we are dealing with proprietary law; if the object of a law serves the action (or abstention from action) of another party, but the subject of the law may only demand that an agreed action be completed (or abstention from the action), then this is contractual law.** In other words, various civil legal relations correspond to defined groups of objects of civil rights. From this perspective, differentiation between property and contractual laws holds great significance, as it predetermines the differences in legal conditions for concrete objects.

Unfortunately, nowadays attempts to merge the different legal procedures are not uncommon. Instead of onerous concessions of rights, attempts are made to «buy and sell» «uncertificated securities», and to consider shareholders as «holders of rights» to shares and «to rent interest in land»[1].

The classification of property rights into proprietary and contractual is not referred to among Roman lawyers, who spoke only of the differences of property suits (actiones in rem) and personal actions (actiones in personam). The differentiation between proprietary and contractual laws was worked out later by legal experts, though based on the materials that Roman lawyers had had. Nevertheless, the latter paid attention to the fact that **the legal position of a party holding proprietary rights to an article and the legal position of a party entering into an agreement with the owner of an article to the effect that the latter is obliged to give him the article for temporary use are not the same.** In the first case, the owner has the opportunity to directly exert influence on the article — to use it, destroy it, transfer it to another party, and so on ('directly' in the sense of independently from any other party). In the

---

[1] *E.A. Sukhanov.* Civil Law. Vol. 1. Moscow, 1998. P. 297 (*Суханов Е.А.* Гражданское право. Т. 1. М., 1998. С. 297).

second case, the debtor's rights to the article are limited, firstly by the period of use which he has agreed with the owner (or the time when the latter demands the article, if a concrete period of time has not been stipulated), and, secondly, the need to return the article (that is, he may not destroy or sell it).

The principal difference between the transfer of property rights (the establishment of easement) and a party's acceptance of the obligation to transfer ownership of an article (carry out another action) lies in the fact that **the obligation of one party to grant another ownership of a known article does not immediately create property rights to this article for the other party. Only as a result of fulfilling such an obligation and under other necessary conditions does the party who has acquired the article become its owner.** Only the right to demand transfer of the article springs directly from the obligation. Therefore, the party who bought the article still does not become its owner even on condition of payment of the purchase price. This party only has the right to demand transfer of the article to him, and only becomes the owner after the article has actually been transferred and on the condition that the person who transferred the article had property rights to it.

Thus the difference between proprietary and contractual laws that is accepted in modern civil law, is also found (conditionally) among the Roman lawyers. As a result of this difference in the object of law the difference in defence arises, which Roman lawyers expressed as a **contrast between property and personal actions.** Modern law has come up with two categories to express this idea: absolute and relative (Table 1).

This idea is based on the following principle: legal relations for ownership of material goods by specific parties have an **absolute nature** — the authorised holder of right is in opposition, so to speak, to an undefined group of individuals (by all other parties) who are obliged to refrain from any infringements of the law against his property and not to hinder the realisation of his rights. The Roman legal experts also considered that, since the object of proprietary interest is a physical item and anyone can encroach upon it, **proprietary interest must be defended against every infringer of the law,** whoever it may be; proprietary interest is used as an absolute defence against a personal action.

In contractual law, a party may request an individual or several precisely defined individuals to execute a particular action. Therefore,

Table 1

Comparison of proprietary and contractual rights

Criterion	Proprietary interest	Law of obligation
Object	Article	Right to demand execution of an action (or abstention from it)
Influence of the right-possessing party	Direct	Request for influence
Nature of legal relations	Absolute — with regard to everything	Relative — with regard to a strictly defined party or group of individuals
Number of rights with regard to object of law	Trio of competences: Instruction Ownership Use	Single competence: Request for defined action to be executed
Status of object of law	Complex: Belongs to X In possession of Y Used by Z	Simple: Exists or does not exist (logically — 1 or 0)
Period of legal relations	Indefinite (perpetual)	Definite (as a rule)

infringers of contractual law are either one party or several specific parties, against whom the subject of the law may bring a personal action. Here, **protection of contractual law is of a relative nature.**

Having rented out a material object, the owner does not lose his property rights to it. When intangible and immaterial receivables are transferred, the creditor simply «quits», his relationship to this right ceases, he completely withdraws from the legal relations.

Both in Roman and modern civil law, from the very beginning, a contractual legal relationship was seen at its natural end as a means of fulfilling a certain action within the fixed deadline. It differs in this way from property rights, established for an indefinite, extended period of time. In cases where a debtor deliberately does not fulfil his duties, the creditor is granted legitimate means, that is, established by law, of compulsorily realising his right of demand. Such a method of forcing the debtor to satisfy the demands of the creditor under a commitment in Rome was a personal action or forced penalty. Ancient Roman lawyers also defined a debtor as a party who whose debt could be recovered against his will.

Legal standards are a particular kind of judgement. Their content reflects the wishes of a legislator in that duty of fulfilment about which there is no doubt. In this sense, legal standards are true judgements. But a judgement with internal necessity turns into a deduction which is used to justify the judgement. «The transition of a judgement into a deduction, which is a justification of its grounds, is a synthetic link, a definite system of seniority, which is also a logical development»[1].

Situations that arise in the course of the logical development of normative judgements must obviously also not provoke doubt with regard to wishes concluded in them. The will and intention of a legislator, developed as a chain reaction — «judgement-deduction-judgement» — are as reliable as their primary element — the standard of law, although we must still always proceed from the fact that in publishing a normative act, a legislator has thought through all its logical and factual consequences and conclusions at which a body that applies the law may arrive.

Drawing from the definitions:
* an entity is an object belonging to the material world;
* an obligation is the right to request a certain person to carry out certain actions or to refuse to do so.

The right to request is immaterial; an entity, material.

Speaking in terms of logic, **many entity-objects and liability-objects do not overlap, or the application of property or contractual legal standards are mutually exclusive.**

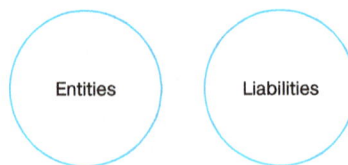

Entities   Liabilities

Using the following logical symbols — ∃ means 'exists', ∀ means 'for any', ∅ means 'empty set', ∈ means 'goes into', ∉ means 'does not go into', ∩ means 'overlap', e means 'entity', E means 'set of entities',

[1] *S.B. Tsereteli* On the system of logical development of idea forms // *Voprosy philosophii.* 1967. Issue 2. Р. 79 (*Церетели С.Б.* О системе логического развития форм мысли // Вопросы философии. 1967. № 2. С. 79).

o means 'obligation/liability', and O means 'set of obligations/liabilities', we shall note:

$$E \cap O = \varnothing \qquad (1)$$
$$(\forall e \in E)\ (e \notin O) \qquad (2)$$
$$(\forall o \in O)\ (o \notin E) \qquad (3)$$

Correspondingly, the rules of circulation for entities must also be applied to liabilities. Is it really possible to have a right of ownership to a right of demand? Is it really possible to give to whomever the right to temporarily use a right of demand? E. A. Sukhanov believes that «objects of property rights are a narrow concept, encompassing only goods, i.e. items belonging to the material world.»[1]

Either there is a right of demand, or there is not. It can be transferred, but for several people to use such a right at the same time is not possible, since it draws twice as many rights and corresponding obligations without agreement with the creditor upon a commitment.

Dualism of proprietary law and contractual law is caused by the absolute non-identity of an article and a person.

There are principal differences in the treatment of objects and liabilities.

Property rights, ownership, holding property, and instruction to right of demand cannot exist, as the right is not a material object.

Personal actions are not applied to obligations, and suits forcing fulfilment are not applied to goods, as goods cannot be compelled to do anything — they are not spiritual beings.

In institutionalism and neo-institutionalism, the position conveyed by Coase prevails, that on the market, material goods themselves do not circulate, but rather bundles of rights to them, and it is precisely these bundles of rights that reveal the real relations between economic subjects in regards to material goods.

Let's consider some examples of the formation of bundles of rights with a monetary loan as an obligation and as an article.

An example of the formation of a bundle of rights with a monetary loan as an obligation.

---

[1] *E.A. Sukhanov.* Objects of property law // *Law*, 1995. Issue 4. P. 94 (*Суханов Е.А.* Объекты права собственности // Закон. 1995. № 4. С. 94).

Let us assume that a certain X borrowed 100 US dollars from Y in non-cash form for a term of five days and lost them on the second day. On the third day X borrowed 80 euro from Z in non-cash form for a term of one year (taking an exchange rate of 1 dollar to 0.8 euro). On the sixth day there are the following legal relations — bundle of rights (Fig. 1):

1) contractual — X is obliged to pay Y 100 US dollars in non-cash form immediately;

2) contractual — X is obliged to pay Z 80 euro in non-cash form in 360 days' time;

3) contractual — the bank is obliged to pay X 80 euro in non-cash form on demand.

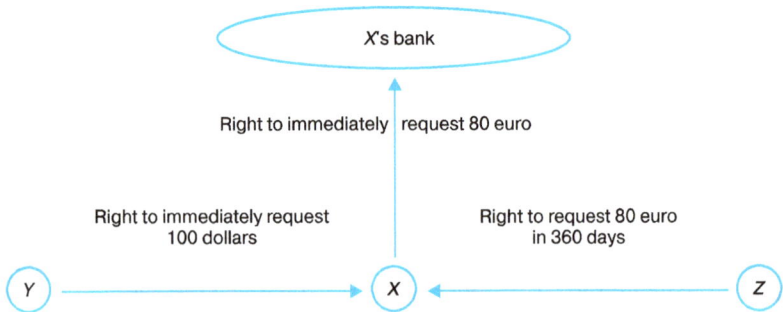

Fig. 1. The legal relations that arise for a loan of money as an obligation

Protecting his rights, Y has the right to demand satisfaction from X's assets, which is expressed in the form of the right of immediate demand to the bank for 80 euro, which the officer of the court on the decision of the court withdraws by coercion from X bank and transfers to Y bank.

Example of the formation of money as an object.

Let us assume that a certain X has borrowed from Y 1 kg of gold in the form of an individually defined bar with Y's stamp for a term of five days and lost it on the second day. On the third day, X borrowed from Z 10 kg of silver in the form of an individually defined bar with Z's stamp for a period of one year (taking an exchange rate of 1 kg gold = 10 kg silver). On the sixth day, when the deadline for payment by X has come, there are the following legal relations — bundle of rights (Fig. 2):

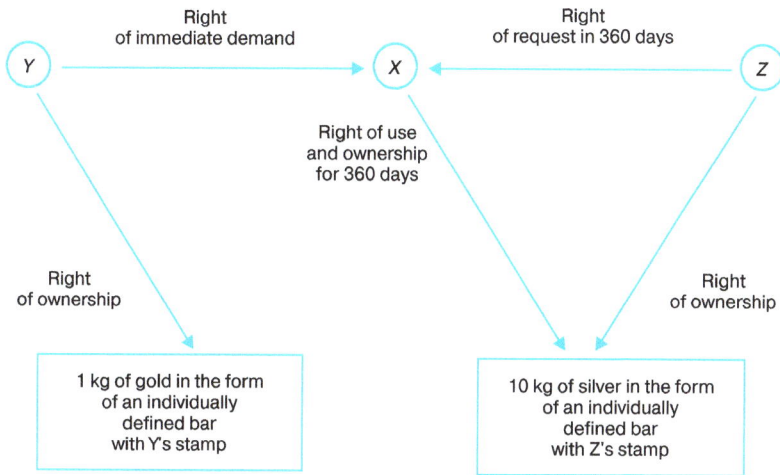

Fig. 2. The legal relations that arise for a loan of money as an object

1) proprietary — *Y* has the right of ownership to 1 kg of gold in the form of an individually defined bar with *Y*'s stamp;

2) contractual — *X* is obliged to give *Y* 1 kg of gold in the form of an individually defined bar with *Y*'s stamp immediately, as the period of temporary ownership and use has elapsed;

3) proprietary — *Z* has the right of ownership to 10 kg of silver in the form of an individually defined bar with *Z*'s stamp;

4) proprietary — *X* has the right to own and use 10 kg of silver in the form of an individually defined bar with *Z*'s stamp for 360 days;

5) contractual — *X* is obliged to give *Z* 10 kg of silver in the form of an individually defined bar with *Z*'s stamp in 360 days' time.

Protecting his rights, *Y* does not have the right to demand satisfaction from *X*'s assets, which are expressed in the form of 10 kg of silver in the form of an individually defined bar with *Z*'s stamp, since the right of ownership to these 10 kg of silver belongs only to *Z*, and nobody except the owner has the right to remove this article from *X*[1].

---

[1] To reassure the reader, let's say that *Y* has the right to demand payment from *X* on account of the goods or other rights belonging to *X* upon his property right, for example, the right to own and use 10 kg of silver in the form of an individually defined bar with *Z*'s stamp for another 360 days.

These examples demonstrate the formation of different bundles of rights and the difference in handling money in proprietary and contractual form, thus showing that different forms of treatment exist for different forms of money.

Part II
SECURITIES

Definition of the problem

It must be noted that the essence and nature of securities are being examined exclusively for future use in the definition of the essence and nature of forms of money such as banknotes and coins with nominal value.

In Russia's working legislation, there is no simple definition of the concepts of «money» and «securities». Neither is there a precise indication of which rights — proprietary or contractual — must be applied in relation to them. Although Article 128 of the CC RF states that «goods including money and securities belong to objects of civil rights...», several instances where this norm is contradicted are to be found in the texts of the CC RF and other laws.

Here are a few examples.

1. In the comments on Article 128 of the CC RF it is written that «goods are material objects of the outside world»[1]. From this comment it follows that so-called non-cash money and uncertificated securities, defined in Article 149 of the CC RF, which do not exist in material form, for precisely this reason cannot be goods. However, on the other hand, Article 128 of the CC RF makes no difference between paper securities and non-documentary ones, putting both in the category of goods, which is incorrect.

2. Paragraph 3, Article 302 of the CC RF denies the possibility of using replevin in relation to bearer money and securities: «Bearer money and securities may not be obtained on demand from a conscientious acquirer.» But according to the law any right of ownership is protected by replevin. It turns out that one of the most important actions in rem does not apply to money and bearer securities, which forces one to doubt the correctness of their being attributed to the category of goods.

---

[1] Commentary on the Civil Code of the RF, Part I / Resp. editor O. N. Sadikov. Moscow, 1995. P. 179.

3. Paragraph 2, Article 144 of the CC RF states: «The absence of obligatory/binding properties of a security or the disparity of a security with form established for it implies its worthlessness». But how can an object be worthless? This concept is only applied to an obligation/liability.

4. In paragraph 2 of Article 147 of the CC RF it is claimed that «refusal to fulfil an obligation, a certified security, with regard to a lack of grounds to the obligation or to its invalidity, is not allowed». This is a direct indication of the contractual, and not proprietary, nature of a security.

5. In Article 816 of the CC RF it is written that «in cases that are provided for by a law or other legal acts, a loan agreement can be concluded by means of the issue and sale of bonds.» This indicates the contractual, and not proprietary, nature of a security.

6. If a security is an entity (according to Article 128 of the CC RF), and a share is a security (according to Article 143 of the CC RF), then a share is an entity. However, Article 48 of the CC RF defines the relationship of participants to the property of an economic society as contractual.

7. If a bill (B) is a security (according to Article 143 of the CC RF) and a bill is an obligation (according to the Convention on a uniform law on derivative and simple shares and Article 815 of the CC RF), then some securities are obligations, which contradicts Article 128 of the CC RF, which classifies securities as entities.

As the rules of an international agreement take priority over the rules of an internal agreement (paragraph 4, Article 15 of the Constitution of the Russian Federation, Article 815 of the CC RF), Article 128 of the CC RF contradicts the legislation in terms of attributing promissory notes, like securities, to entities.

Accepting the logical evidence, it can be established (**B** — bill, **S** — security) that:

$$\mathbf{B} \in \mathbf{O}, \tag{4}$$

i.e. a bill belongs to the set of obligations (source — Convention on a uniform law on derivative and simple shares);

$$\mathbf{B} \in \mathbf{S}, \tag{5}$$

i.e. a bill belongs to the set of securities; consequently,

$$\mathbf{O} \subset \mathbf{S}, \tag{6}$$

i.e. the set of obligations and the set of securities overlap; consequently, by induction

$$\exists\, \mathbf{s} \in \mathbf{O}, \tag{7}$$

i.e. there are some securities that belong in the set of obligations and

$$\exists\, \mathbf{o} \in \mathbf{S}, \tag{8}$$

i.e. there are some obligations which belong in the set of securities (are obligations/liabilities).

Securities — Promissory notes — Liabilities

However, based on Article 128 of the CC RF:

$$\forall\, \mathbf{s} \in \mathbf{E}, \tag{9}$$

i.e. any security is an entity.

Then from the fact that

$$\exists\, \mathbf{o} \in \mathbf{S}, \tag{8}$$

and

$$\forall\, \mathbf{s} \in \mathbf{E}, \tag{9}$$

it follows that:

$$\exists\, \mathbf{o} \in \mathbf{E}, \tag{10}$$

i.e. there are some obligations that belong to the set of entities, which contradicts the following:

$$\forall\, \mathbf{o} \notin \mathbf{E},$$

i.e. any obligation does not belong in the set of entities (see (3)).

Then we see that (4) contradicts (9), and in conflict (4) is higher than (9).

Therefore, assertion (9) is false.

8. Knowing that non-cash money is a liability, and not an entity, we reach the logical verdict that:

• ownership is only a proprietary category;

• for a loan (Article 807 of the CC RF), money is transferred into the ownership of the debtor;

_____by deduction_____
Article 807 of the CC RF (loan) regulates only the loan of goods (not liabilities);

non-cash money is not an entity (but a liability);

_____by deduction_____
Article 807 of the CC RF (loan) does not regulate relations with non-cash money

and

• ownership is only a proprietary category;

for commercial credit (Article 823 of the CC RF), money is transferred into the ownership of another party;

_____by deduction_____
Article 823 of the CC RF (commercial credit) regulates only the commercial credit of an entity;

Article 823 of the CC RF (commercial credit) does not regulate commercial credit of non-cash money.

9. Why is a loan agreement (contract) an obligation, whereas bonds are an entity? After all, they express practically the same content and differ only in form.

10. Having traced the history of the development of literal contracts (receipts), we can see that the development of circulation transformed them into promissory notes. But in Roman law, literal contracts were related to contractual law, while the CC RF applies property law to promissory notes (like a type of security).

So which laws and actions can we use in relation to securities? If the answer is proprietary, that means that there is a right of ownership for securities and personal actions can be applied to them. But if securities are recognised as an obligation, then property law and personal actions for securities are not suitable, but rather receivables and actions characteristic of liabilities are applicable.

Definitions of securities
in legislation outside Russia

*Nobody has yet succeeded in understanding the notion of
securities either in life, in science, or in legislation.*

G. F. Shershenevich

In *common law* there is no precise definition of the essence of a security; only unifying concepts of securities are given.

The UK

The term «securities» means stocks, securities and shares (*Settled
Land Act,* 1925, paragraph 117).

As applied to a legal entity, «securities» means all types of shares,
share capital, bonds, preferred shares and other securities of a similar
type, which are used by legal entities (*Transport Act,* 1962, paragraph 92).

«Securities» is understood to mean shares, share capital, bonds,
preferred shares, loan capital, promissory notes, or a share in a collec-
tive investment scheme, in accordance with the provisions of the *Financial Services Act,* 1986, and other types of securities (*Stock Transfer
Act,* 1963, paragraph 4, taking into account the provisions of the *Financial Services Act,* 1986.

'The main meaning of the word «securities» is not open to doubt.
The word denotes a debt or claim the payment of which is in some way
secured. The security would generally consist of a right to resort to some
fund or property for payment, although in this case we can exclude
other forms of debt (particularly guarantees offered by a physical person). Nevertheless, in any specific case, the use of the word or phrase
in its main sense provides for some form of secured liability (Singer V.
Williams [1921] AC 41, 49, HNL, per Viscont Cave).

The USA

The term «security» is understood to mean all types of promissory
notes, share capital, treasury shares, guarantees, evidence of debt,
certificates attesting to the owner's share in a company's revenue or
participation in any kinds of agreements on division of profit, certificates of the guarantee of other companies by securities, certificates of

preliminary agreements or subscription certificates (provisional sub-scription certificates), transferred shares, investment contracts, voting trust certificates, indivisible share participation relating to rights to extract oil, gas and other useful minerals or all types of interest or means of payment as a whole, known as «debt security», or certificates attest-ing to the owner's share in a company's revenue or his participation in any provisional certificates, receipts, guarantees or rights to subscrip-tion or acquisition of any of the aforementioned obligations (*Securities Act*, 1933, paragraph 2 (1)).

A rather incomprehensible definition of the essence of a security is to be found in the Uniform Commercial Code of the USA (para-graph (c), pages 8–102):

«A security is either documentary or non-documentary. If a secu-rity is documentary, the terms «security» and «documentary security» can mean either an **intangible property interest, or a document which represents such an interest,** or both of these depending on the con-text.»

Other countries

Germany's Civil Code and Trade Code do not contain a clear defi-nition of a security.

Only in the Code of Property Law of the Swiss Confederation is there a more-or-less decent definition of the essence of a security (Ar-ticle 965):[1]

«A security is any document to which a right is related in such a way that one cannot lay claim to it and one cannot transfer it to another party without said document».

---

[1] Artikel 965 des Schweizerischen Obligationenrechts // http://www.admin.ch/ch/d/sr/220/a965.html

Securities as an economic category and legislative treatment of them

Entities are not simply material objects, but material objects whose source of value is their natural useful properties. The source of value of documents[1] (including securities) is information, that is, social rather than natural qualities.

V.A. Byelov

The origin of securities as a particular object of property turnover is linked to the historical period when people needing to transfer large quantities of goods and money were faced with a lack of economically justified means to make such a transfer.

Lawyers found a solution as long ago as 6–5 B.C., when they had the sense to convert the very documents that certified concrete transactions into a special kind of commodity, a special value system, that coincided neither with goods in the proper sense of the word nor with money. Until transaction documents were completed in the form of clay or wax tablets, or on papyrus or parchment, they were not widely in circulation.

Paper was invented in the 6th century in China, and in the 9th and 10th centuries, its method of production became known in Western Europe. It was then, under conditions of a natural economy and feudal division, a long way away from a market economy, that paper documents concerning concrete transactions received general recognition and distribution as a particular object of economic circulation.

Types of securities

Securities are shares, bonds, promissory notes and other (including derivative) certificates of property rights (rights to resources), which have been separated from their basis and are recognised in this capacity by legislation.

The federal law dated 29 April 1996 No. 39-FL «On the securities market» specifies that «...a security...is characterised... by the following indicators: **it secures the aggregate of property and non-property rights** subject to certification, concession and unconditional execution in accordance with the forms and order established by this federal law».

---

[1]   Including agreements (contracts)

There is also a definition of a security in Article 142 of the CC RF: «**A security is a document**[1] that certifies...**property rights**...».

However, it follows from this that there is a mistake in Article 128 of the CC RF, which places securities among goods, as a document which reflects a law of obligation vested in it is an obligation, but not an object.

In paragraph 2 of Article 147 of the CC RF, the contractual nature of securities is directly referred to: «Refusal to fulfil an **obligation certified by a security**, with reference to the obligation's lack of foundation or its invalidity, is prohibited».

We understand goods to mean material objects of the external world. They include both objects of material and spiritual culture, that is, products of human labour, and objects created by nature itself and used by people in their life's work — land, useful minerals, plants, and so on.

The most important characteristic of goods, due to which they are also becoming objects of civil law, is their capacity to satisfy all sorts of human needs.

Each type of legal relations with different types of property, as a rule, corresponds to its own type of security, which in turn can play a part in civil transactions (Table 2).

There are dozens of types of securities. They are distinguishable by the rights and obligations, which are vested in them, of the creditor (purchaser of the security) and the issuer of the securities. However, not all of them are distinguished when reflected in business accounts (a few types of securities that have similar features can be singled out).

In accordance with Article 143 of the CC RF, the following count as securities:

---

[1] Federal Law No. 77-FL on legal deposit copy of documents, dated 29 December 1994, defines a document as «a material bearer with information stated in it in the form of a text, sound recording (phonogram), image or combinations of these, designed to be broadcast in time and space for the purposes of public use and storage» (Article 1). Federal Law No. 149-FL on information, information technology and the protection of information, dated 27 July 2006, states that «documentary information is stated in a material bearer by means of documentation of information with properties which allow the definition of such information or, in cases established by the legislation of the Russian Federation, its material bearer...» (Article 2).

Table 2

Correspondence of types of property and securities

Types of resources	Corresponding securities
Land	Mortgage (mortgage certificate), shares in land
Real estate	Mortgage, privatisation voucher, housing certificate
Production	Bill of lading, circulating warehouse certificate
Money	Bond, banknote, promissory note, deposit or savings certificate, cheque, etc.
Stock	Shares (ordinary, privileged) Derivative securities — derivatives (indices, options, futures)

1) government stock;

2) bonds;

3) promissory notes;

4) cheques;

5) deposit and savings certificates;

6) savings bank books payable to the bearer;

7) bills of lading;

8) shares;

9) privatisation securities;

10) other documents which fall into the category of securities according to laws on securities or order established by such laws.

Bond — this is a security that certifies the right of the holder to receive from the party that issued the obligation, within the specified period, the nominal value of the bond or some material equivalent. A bond also grants its holder the right to receive the interest stated in it on the nominal value of the bond or other proprietary interest (Article 816 of the CC RF). A bond can provide for other proprietary interest of the holder, if this does not contradict the legislation of the Russian Federation. Bonds can be issued by the State, and by private companies in order to raise loan capital (Article 2 of Federal Law No. 39-FL on the securities market, dated 22 April 1996). Bonds provided by a mortgage give their holders an additional guarantee against loss of their funds, as a mortgage gives the owner of the bonds the right to sell mortgaged property in the event that a company is not in the position to realise due payments. However, unsecured bonds also exist, which are debt securities based only on trust in the credit rating of a company, but not guaranteed by any property. Such bonds are issued by companies in a stable financial position.

Bill/Promissory note — this document certifies the in no way stipulated obligation of the drawer of the bill (promissory note) or of any other payer mentioned in the bill (bill of exchange) to pay borrowed monies at maturity of the bill (Article 815 of the CC RF).

Cheque — this is a security containing an unspecified order of the issuer to the bank to effect payment to the holder of the cheque of the amount specified in the order. Only the bank where the issuer holds funds, which he is entitled to manage by issuing cheques, can be listed as the cheque payer (Article 877 of the CC RF).

Savings (deposit) certificate — this security certifies the sum of an investment in a bank and the right of the investor (certificate holder) to receive the sum of the investment upon the expiry of a set date as well as the interest, stipulated in the certificate, at the bank which issued the certificate, or at any subsidiary of this bank. Savings (deposit) certificates may be bearer certificates or nominal certificates. In the event of premature presentation of a savings (deposit) certificate for payment by the bank, the sum of the investment and interest are paid for call deposits, if a different rate of interest has not been set by the conditions of the certificate (Article 844 of the CC RF).

Share — this is an equity security which secures the rights of its owner (shareholder) to receive part of the profits of a joint-stock company in the form of dividends, to participate in the management of the company, and to own part of the stock remaining after its liquidation (Article 2 of the Federal Law «On the securities market»).

A whole range of *secondary securities* (*derivatives*) also exists, which secure the rights and obligations of the issuer and the investor in relation to the fulfilment of certain operations with securities. This kind of securities includes options, futures and indices.

Option — this is a short-term security, which grants its owner the right to buy or sell another security during a specified period for a fixed price to a contracting party which, for a price, takes on the obligation to realise this right.

Financial futures — these are standard short-term contracts for the purchase or sale of a certain security for a fixed price on a fixed date in the future. If the owner of an option may waive his right, having lost the cash bonus which he paid to the contracting agent, then the futures contract is compulsory for the subsequent performance.

Characteristics of securities

In accordance with the law and customary business practices, a document which certifies title of ownership and which meets the following requirements is usually recognised as a security:

* negotiability;
* availability for civil transactions;
* commonality of forms and properties.

Negotiability — this is the capacity of a security to independently participate in civil-legal transactions through simplified procedure, for example, by performing an endorsement or simple transfer of a bearer security (Article 146 of the CC RF).

Negotiability indicates that a security exists as a special commodity which, consequently, must have its own market with organisation distinctive to it, codes of practice, and so on. Most of those resources, whose owners' rights are reflected by securities, must also belong to the market as goods.

Availability for civil transactions means that a security must represent title of ownership: for example, commodity circulation of weapons, pharmaceuticals, and so on is restricted.

Commonality means that a security must have clearly standardised properties that are defined by law (face value, place of issue, etc.). It is precisely this which simplifies the circulation of goods and gives it State protection.

N. O. Nersesov on securities

The founder of Russian theory on securities, N. O. Nersesov, wrote at the end of the 19th century:

«Bearer securities (*Inhaberpapiere, les titres au porteur*) comprise one type of securities. Therefore an account of the study of bearer securities would be a useful preface to some preliminary words on the legal nature of securities in general. The very term «securities» (*Werthpapiere, les valeurs* or *les effets*) until now has not had a precise definition, either in spoken language or in legislation. Additional terms are needed to describe the concept of securities, such as interest-bearing, credit, monetary and commodity securities. But none of these are notable for their accuracy. Not every security bears a particular interest, like, for example, a bill of lading, invoice, warrant certificate, tickets for travel by rail and sea, theatre and concert tickets, and so on. In other words, not every security is *interest-bearing*. Furthermore, not all securities are based exclusively on an obligation, i.e. they do not all grant the legal owner the right of demand from a particular debtor; as do shares, for example. Consequently, the term «*credit* securities» does not embrace all types of securities.

There is a multitude of securities of which the subject is not a specific sum of money, but rather some kind of entity — such as all the traditional securities: bill of lading, invoice, warrant certificate; therefore, the term «*monetary* securities is not a well-founded one. Finally, not every security is at the same time the object of trade transactions, such as, for example, dinner and theatre passes, etc.; thus the term «*commodity* securities» also proves to be inaccurate.

In legal literature the term «securities» is fairly widely used, especially from the second half of this (19th — *note by the Editor*) century onwards. But there is much disagreement among lawyers on the question of the concept of these securities. Some confine the concept of securities to order securities and nameless securities; others include registered securities (*Rectapapiere*), such as, for example, nominal shares. Some exclude passenger tickets, dinner passes, entrance tickets to public shows, etc., from the concept of securities. Hahn, a commentator on the German Civil Code, even includes paper money and postage stamps in the category of securities. Famous commercialist Thol considers securities to be any documents with proprietary-legal content, so in this he includes a freight letter, a broker's note and a loan obligation. Endemann regards securities as representatives of value (*Werthtrager*). According to him, the security itself has no real value, like any other physical object, but is a bearer of value. The value is based on trust that the debtor (the issuer of the document) will fulfil his promise. Therefore, the value of similar document is based on credit. Endemann counts as securities, among others, State paper currency, which is also a representative of value, as it embodies the opportunity to be realised (exchanged for metal coins) in the future.

The most widespread definition is that **securities are an obligation embodied in a document** (*verkörperte Forderungsrechte*). Brunner opposes this definition. He says that rights cannot have a body in which they are personified. Following this theory, one has to distinguish between corporeal and incorporeal rights (*körperliche und unkörperliche Rechte*). But Brunner's observation is more witty than essentially correct. In saying that an obligation is embodied in a document, lawyers aim to point out the close link between the law and the document, and the considerable significance of this for the law that results from it, an idea which Brunner himself expresses in his final pages.

Knies' definition differs in its comparatively high precision. Having analysed the distinguishing features of securities, he arrives, finally, at the following descriptive definition: **a security exists when a right is so closely linked with a document that its owner may demand realisation from the counter party.** Just as ownership of an object is transferred through the extradition of said object, so the right of demand to a specified sum of money or a certain commodity in another's possession changes through the transfer of a security whose contents consists of the cited sum of money or commodity.

There is a similar discrepancy in opinions due to the lack of a precise definition of the legal nature of securities. The majority of lawyers either do not dwell on this question at all, or give an imprecise definition.

Essential characteristics of securities

Instead of giving a definition of securities in several words, we shall point out their essential characteristics.

Securities become such as a result of the right that lies in the document. The document itself has no value (not taking into account the material, of course); the value only comes from the right which the document expresses. Therefore, the essence of securities is that connection that exists between said right and the document.

Therefore, **the first essential feature in the concept of securities is that they are documents about individual rights**[1]. A document concern-

---

[1] The author believes that a security can also define public law (a government bond is an obligation of the Ministry of Finance).

ing civil law can have threefold significance: the establishment, transfer or realisation of a right. A document by means of which a *right is
established* may, in turn, have double significance: either it serves as a
simple means of proof, a surface form of the legal act, or it has considerable significance for the origin of this right (*corpus negotii*), as
without the document there is no right. It is essential for the concept
of securities that a right is closely linked with the document, and that
ownership of the document is considered a necessary condition for
the accomplishment of the aim for which the document serves. It
follows from this that a document, as simple proof of the establishment of such legal relations, cannot be regarded as a security, if only
realisation or transfer of the right are not granted through ownership
of the document.

Thus it is essential for the concept of a security that a document has
considerable significance either for the origin, or the transfer, or the
realisation of the right.

**Securities arise principally in the interests of facilitating the transfer-
ability or realisation of a right,** but attention can also be drawn to a type
of security in which the aspect of circulatability is lacking: for example,
nominal shares, the transfer of which is normally carried out according
to the principles of *cessio*. Nevertheless, they are securities, because
ownership of the document is considered an essential aspect in the
matter of using the right associated with that share. This can also be
said of other types of registered documents of commodity circulation
(*Rectapapiere*).

The abovementioned essential aspect of the concept of securities
(with the ownership of a document, the realisation of its rights are
begun) determines the following logical consequences.

1. The property of the creditor in relation to securities is based on
the moment of *formal* legitimisation, that is, the creditor is considered
to be whoever has ownership of the document, and ownership, in turn,
is governed by legitimate possession of the document. Legitimate possession here is the irrefutable assumption of the rights of ownership
(*praesumptio juris et de jure*). The debtor, fulfilling his obligations in the
name of the owner, is freed from further responsibility, although it
subsequently proved that the document passed to the owner not from
the proprietor. The latter has only a personal action against the direct

infringer of his rights. For example, a depository sold bearer securities that were in his custody or got reparation for them from the debtor. In the first case, the rights of ownership to the document and the rights linked to it are transferred to the bona fide purchaser, and in the second case, the debtor is definitively freed from further responsibility. The depositor, whose interests were infringed by similar actions of the depository, may seek damages only from the latter as a direct infringer of his rights.

2. Securities cannot be liable to vindication in accordance with the principles of civil law. The very use of vindications for securities has a different meaning, as the objective of such a replevin is not the return of the document as such, but the recovery of the rights closely linked with it. Moreover, the rigorism of this regulation is relaxed by special decree of positive legislation.

3. In the event that a document is lost or destroyed, the right connected with it must also discontinue. Positive legislation makes it possible in such cases to recreate the previous status through amortisation or cancellation of the lost document and payments in exchange for a duplicate.

4. Document ownership is also considered a necessary condition for transfer of the right to it, regardless of whether it is a matter of transferring rights of ownership or of establishing a mortgage right»[1].

Securities as unilateral contracts

In essence a security is none other than a **unilateral contract[2] concluded in a single copy, in which one of the parties may be changed without the agreement of the other party (freely traded obligation).** «Let us note that negotiability is a very important legal characteristic. The difference between a traded security (bond, promissory note) and a simple debt payment lies in the lack of formalities such as notification of the debtor. The purchaser conscientiously, for a price, acquires the legal

---

[1] *N.O. Nersesov.* Representation and securities in civil law. Moscow, 1998. P. 138–142 (*Нерсесов Н.О.* Представительство и ценные бумаги в гражданском праве. М., 1998. С. 138–142).

[2] A security must be regarded as a unilateral contract, as the will of only one side — the issuer — is needed for its issue, while another side — the holder — is needed for its circulation.

title of holder of the traded security, which is free of any defects. By contrast, a simple assignor of a debt acquires only such a title as was actually held by the assignee, and is subject to any actions of third parties.

Thus circulatability ensures «pure» relations between each subsequent holder of the security and the issuer»[1].

In support of this theoretical premise of circulatability, the CC RF claims that **rights cannot be certified by a security that is inextricably linked with the identity of the creditor,** particularly claims for alimony and reimbursement of damages caused to life and health.

Jhering states that a bearer security is only legally a secure means of establishing (*Begrundung*) an obligation[2].

Nersesov quotes the theory of a unilateral promise as the source of bearer securities: «Securities arise due to the one-sided actions of a debtor, who prepares a document, signs it and in so doing creates a new value. The conditions of validity of the document must be served exclusively on behalf of the debtor. However, the document, while it remains in the hands of the debtor, does not have value, it is only a piece of paper, and only acquires value upon transfer into the hands of another. The wishes of the latter (the acquirer) are circumstantial and play a subsidiary role or, rather, this second aspect is a condition (*conditio*) under which said security acquires legal validity. Thus the document as such is considered valid due to the will of the debtor unilaterally represented in it, but its practical effect is frozen until it passes into the hands of the acquirer»[3].

The evolution of contracts into securities

Particular attention should be paid to the fact that such contracts are unilateral only and in them the issuer always gives the obligation, while the holder is always the «creditor». It is important to note that real contracts of this type can instantly be drawn up in the form of a security, whereas consensual contracts are presented in such a form as

---

[1] Clifford Chance: Review of the issue of Eurobonds. 1997. March.
[2] *N. O. Nersesov*. Aforementioned work. P. 201 (*Нерсесов Н.О.* Указ. соч. С. 201).
[3] Ibidem. P. 200.

a result of the fulfilment by the «creditor»-holder of his (usually first) obligation.

From our reasoning we arrive at the diagram shown in Fig. 3, from which it follows that:

* a share is a document that forms an actual contract on pooling of capital after a shareholder's deposit of money or other valuables, in which the shareholder party may change without the agreement of the other side (issuer) — a legal party in the form of a joint-stock company;

* a bond is an actual loan agreement of objects of law — money, where the creditor party may change without the agreement of the borrower (issuer);

* a warrant certificate is an actual storage contract where the warrant holder may change without the agreement of the (issuer) warrant giver;

* a bill of lading is, in its own way, a «transport» storage contract, which differs from a warrant certificate in regard to the place of storage: it is an object of transport (ship, train, aeroplane, etc.), travelling in time and space;

* a bill/promissory note is an abstract literal contract, where the bill holder (creditor) may change without the agreement of the bill giver (issuer) by means of an endorsement, and the borrower can change without the agreement of the holder by means of acceptance (sometimes collateral security).

Section IV of the CC RF, «Individual types of obligations», corroborates this, stating that **securities certify property rights resulting from contracts** including loan agreements (Articles 815–817), bank deposit agreements (Article 844), cheque payment contracts (Article 877) and warehouse storage agreements (Article 912).

It should be noted that rights certified by a security are never corporeal, but are always of a contractual nature, as they define legal relations between two parties.

«Bearer securities are literal contracts of modern law»[1].

«A transfer note, *assignatio* and other such legal relations also recognised by our legislation demonstrate the possibility of acquisition by

---
[1] *N. O. Nersesov.* Aforementioned work. P. 199.

Action of creditors				Consensual contract — company
Classical (Roman) bilateral contract				Deposit of money by share-holder
Obligation in the form of unilateral contract	Literal contract (abstract)	Actual contract on pooling of capital	Actual contract — loan	Actual contract — storage
Obligation in the form of a security one of the parties (sometimes both) may change — FREELY TRADED OBLIGATION	Bill/ Promissory note — formal obligation (does not contain considera-tions)	Share	Bond	Warrant certificate	Transport warrant certifi-cate — bill of lading

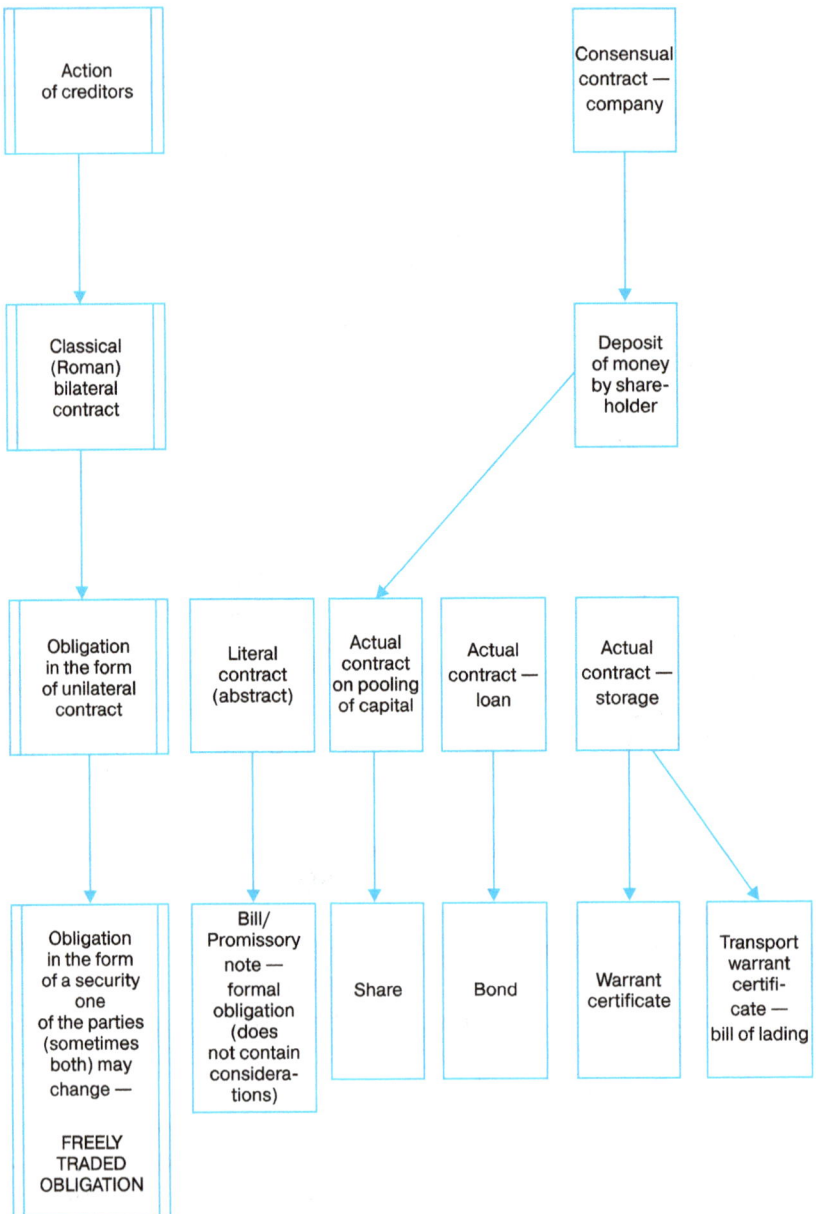

Fig. 3. The evolution of contracts into securities

an outside party of the right of demand from a contract concluded by others»[1].

The emergence of securities simplified the certification of ownership of rights to a defined entity (legitimisation). Legitimisation using a security must be accomplished exclusively by formal methods, which obliges one not to take into account any other circumstances, even those that discredit the owner of a document (therein lies the feature of public reliability of a security). **In relation to a security, the debtor does not have the right to verify whether the party demanding fulfilment is his creditor.** In order to free himself from responsibility associated with the security, the debtor must fulfil the requirement of the party that is responsible according to the officially established formal indicators.

So, powers in relation to a bearer security belonged to its actual owner, while powers for registered and order securities belonged to the owner of the corresponding document with an indication of the owner as the first acquirer or endorsee (originally registered securities, as a rule, could be transferred using endorsements on general foundations with order securities). Therefore to transfer rights it was necessary only to complete the procedure required and sufficient for future legitimisation of the acquirer of rights before the debtor for a security. Such a transfer could take place by means of a simple delivery of the document (security with or without an endorsement) to the acquirer of rights.

Bearer securities as complex legal relations

In any registered (order) security, the holder is defined by an indication of an individual sign of the party — name or title (sometimes address). **Only in a bearer security the bearer's right of ownership signifies the right to make demands to the issuer — and this is an exceptional case.** The second paragraph of Article 142 of the CC RF is only applied in this exceptional case: «With the transfer of a security, all of its rights are transferred in aggregate», because in an unethical transfer of a registered security, rights of claim towards the issuer remain with the previous holder of the security.

---

[1] *Ibidem.* P. 146.

But even in this exceptional case, there is an argument for recognising a bearer security as an obligation. The fact is that the very word for bill/promissory note in Russian — вексель (vieksiel) — arrived in the Russian language from German, in which it is pronounced very similarly — *Wechsel*. The primary meaning of the word *Wechsel* is *exchange*. In this case it is translated as «exchange document», «that which can be changed». And, of course, in English it is translated as *promissory note*. Thus, in the English language, the very concept of the promissory note is formed from the nature of an object, and a ready-made foreign (German) name arrived in Russia, which did not disclose its nature.

By analysing this problem a little more thoroughly, we see that a bearer security is a derivative security, the simplest derivative.

Unfortunately, the existence of complex securities is not mentioned in the CC RF, and neither do securities as futures, forwards, converted contracts for the supply of exchange goods, index securities and more complex futures for index securities feature in Russia's legal sphere.

Let us compare the legal relations shown in Figure 4.

«From our definition of unnamed documents, it is clear that the bearer form is the **last step in the historical process of facilitating methods of transfer of obligations.** A lot of time had to pass between the unconditional non-transferability of obligations, which was the case for all peoples at the first level of legal development, and equating them with real objects through bearer forms»[1].

Only in such an exceptional case (bearer securities) is the following opinion justified:

«If we examine unnamed documents at the crucial moments of their existence, i.e. at the beginning (when they come into being) and at the end (when they are satisfied), then they become obligatory relations (*obligatio*); and if we examine them in their period of existence in material turnover (in circulation, negotiations), then they become real objects, like each *res*»[2].

We can note here that when such an «unnamed» security is in circulation, people make use of the rules that are applied to objects, but the nature of these securities nevertheless remains obligatory.

---

[1] *N. O. Nersesov*. Aforementioned work. P. 22.
[2] Ibidem. P. 205.

Registered security:
circulated by endorsement —
simplified session

Complex security:
primary right — claim to issuer;
secondary right — proprietary right
to the object (paper slip).
Circulated in accordance
with the rules of secondary
legal relations, i.e. proprietary.

| Holder (creditor) | Holder (creditor) |

Proprietary law
(possession, ownership, use)

Right of demand

Paper slip

Right of demand

| Issuer (debtor) | Issuer (debtor) |

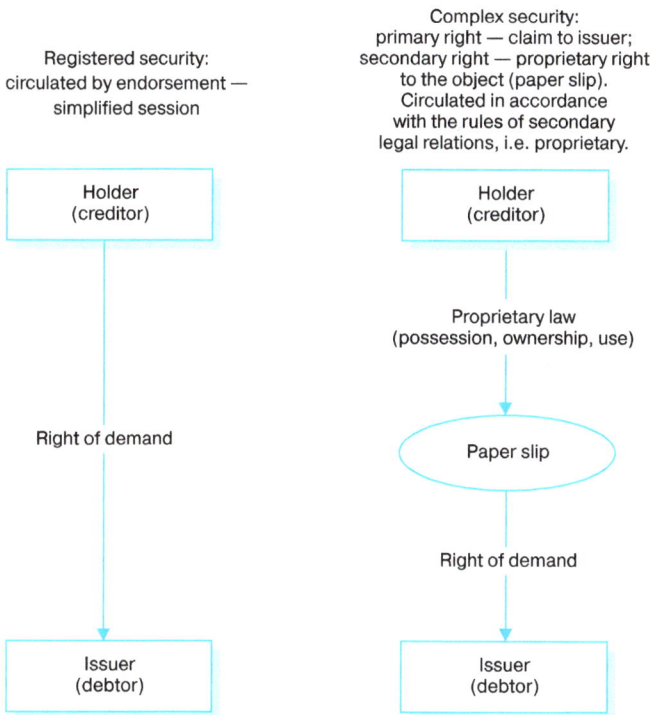

Figure 4. Legal relations that arise through the circulation
of registered and complex securities

«When it is necessary to deal with bearer securities while they are being circulated in civil turnover, the standards of proprietary law must be applied to them. Unnamed documents can be the object of possession, ownership, mortgaging and so on. The right of ownership to them is acquired in the same way as the right of ownership to personal property is acquired. Possession here is assumed at conscientious ownership; this assumption is irrefutable (*praesumptio juris et de jure*). To put it simply, for bearer securities, as for securities in general, one must make a distinction between the *right to a document* and the *right from a document*. The first is provided for by conscientious acquisition of the document, the second, by simple, factual ownership; the first is dealt with in accordance with the rules of proprietary law, and the second in accordance with the rules of law of obligations.

The legal basis of the origin of bearer securities is the unilateral promise of the debtor; in order to acquire the rights from these it is necessary to own the document.

Bearer securities are unilateral formal obligations in circulation, like real entities»[1] (Fig. 5).

«Some institutions of civil law **are, so to speak, caught between proprietary law and law of obligations.** This also relates to bearer securities. By some characteristics they are subject to the definitions of law of obligations, and by others, to proprietary law»[2].

Let it be repeated once again that the above relates to bearer securities only, and in no way applies to registered securities.

Inadequacy of economic nature and modern legislative treatment of securities

«It would not be wrong for us to attribute the main reason for the difference of opinion in the legal nature of unnamed securities to the influence of the prevailing dogma of Roman law. According to the theory of the latter, there is a pronounced difference between the areas of proprietary and contractual law; *res* and *obligatio* are two legal concepts that stand in marked contrast to each other. Counting bearer securities as obligations, German legal experts saw, at the same time, that it was impossible to apply to them all the conclusions of Roman contractual law. Meanwhile, in the law of modern peoples, this marked difference between these areas of civil law does not exist»[3].

The first error in the existing CC RF is the absence of any differentiation between the following laws:

*   obligation — the right of demand, expressed in a security;
*   proprietary interest in the material bearer of the right of demand.

In the overwhelming majority of cases, the value of the material bearer of demand (material object) is incommensurably less than the value of the right of demand (obligation) conveyed in this object. The value of the object can therefore be disregarded, applying the mathematical concept of «little-o». Thus, **it is necessary to imply the right of**

---

[1] *N.O. Nersesov.* Aforementioned work. P. 205.
[2] Ibidem.
[3] *N. O. Nersesov.* Aforementioned work. P. 205.

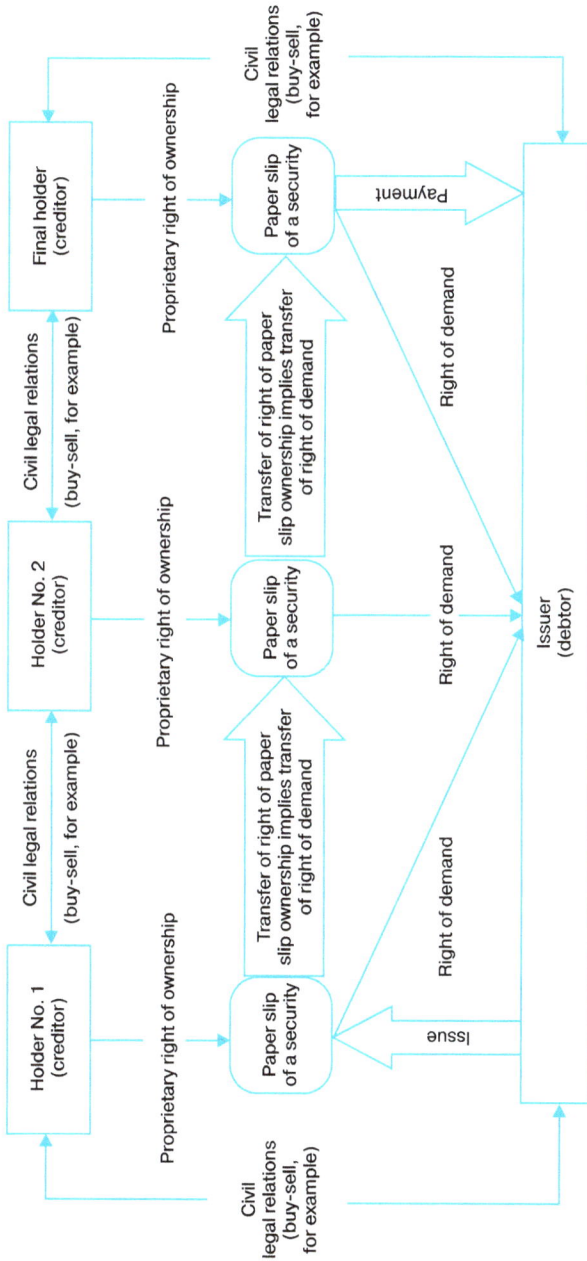

Fig. 5. Circulation of a bearer security (complex legal relations):

primary right — demand to issuer; secondary right — proprietary right to the paper slip; circulated according to the norms of secondary legal relations — proprietary.

demand under the term «security» — a freely traded obligation, expressed through some kind of material bearer (usually paper).

In the legal sense, securities are documents which are valuable, not a material object on the strength of their natural properties, but due to the right to some value that is contained in them.

As D. V. Murzin correctly emphasises, «a security represents value not in itself, even being a material object, but acts as an instrument for the definition of the essence and magnitude of transferred rights»[1].

The second error in the CC RF is the expansion of specific proprietary rules for the treatment of bearer securities to all other securities. Murzin, having analysed the features of securities, arrived at the conclusion that «the concept of the security in part 1, paragraph 1, Article 142 of the CC RF relates, most likely, only to bearer securities, and the exceptions are so prevalent that they make the dogmatic definition itself an exception to the general rule»[2].

According to G. F. Shershenevich, registered securities cannot be called entities[3], while R. Savatier has suggested that only a record in the appropriate books transfers a right that is represented in a registered security[4].

In fact, registered securities are not handled in accordance with the principle of «the right to a document», because the right is precisely consolidated between two clearly defined parties.

The right to a document and the right from a document

The need to make property relations more dynamic led to the appearance of legal constructions which made it possible to include rights in property turnover like real objects. The expression «the right is embodied in the document», or something similar, is usually used to describe this phenomenon. However, M. M. Agarkov believes that «this

---

[1] *D.V. Murzin*. Securities are incorporeal entities. Legal problems with the modern theory of securities. Moscow, 1998. P. 16 (*Мурзин Д.В.* Ценные бумаги — бестелесные вещи. Правовые проблемы современной теории ценных бумаг. М., 1998. С. 16).

[2] Ibidem. P. 30.

[3] *G.F. Shershenevich*. Manual of Russian Civil Law. Moscow, 1995. P. 156 (*Шершеневич Г.Ф.* Учебник русского гражданского права. М., 1995. С. 156).

[4] *R. Savatier*. Theory of obligations. Moscow. 1972. P. 109 (*Саватье Р.* Теория обязательств. М., 1972. С. 109).

formula should not be given greater significance than a figurative expression which does not have the level of precision that is necessary in legal constructions»[1].

L. Enneccerus elaborated thus: «In securities, the right to the paper, as to a document, follows from the right that is expressed in the paper, whereas for bearer securities and order securities, the right coming from the paper comes from the right to the paper, as to a document»[2].

K.I. Sklovsky, describing the historical priority of property rights over contractual rights, remarks: «Contractual rights are used in known cases as a fiction of an entity, forming incorporeal entities and, on this basis, the 'right to a right'»[3].

With regard to the expressions «right to the document» and «right from the document», it ought to be noted that the phrases «right to the medium» and «right from the medium» seem to be more correct when the media can be:

- paper — Europe;
- polymer — Australia, New Zealand, Singapore;
- silk — Central Asia until the last century[4];
- parchment — Ancient China;
- leather — Russia in the 18th century[5];
- clay tablets — Ancient Egypt;
- wax-covered wooden boards — Ancient Rome;
- birchbark documents — Novgorod in the 13th century;
- a section of wall on which the obligation was carved with a chisel;
- a section of asphalt on which the obligation was written in chalk, and so on.

   But computer records, such as:
- non-cash shares in the *NASDAQ* system (USA) and the *RTS* (PTC) system (Russia), and

---

[1] *M.M. Agarkov.A* study of securities. Moscow, 1993 (*Агарков М.М.* Учение о ценных бумагах. М., 1993).

[2] *L. Enneccerus.* Course of German Civil Law. Moscow, 1950. P. 27 (*Эннекцерус Л.* Курс германского гражданского права. М., 1950. С. 27).

[3] *K.I. Sklovsky.* Ownership in Civil Law. Moscow, 1999. P. 57 (*Скловский К.И.* Собственность в гражданском праве. М., 1999. С. 57).

[4] *A.S. Melnikova.* The money of Russia. 1000 years. Moscow, 2000. P. 234 (*Мельникова А.С.* Деньги России. 1000 лет. М., 2000. С. 234).

[5] Ibidem. P. 60.

- traders' obligations to the largest commodity exchanges in the world (conducted through a computer), etc.,

have proprietary expression only for one party — effecting the fixation of property rights — and these records may not be transferred to other parties, because only the owner of the computer that holds information on the medium (hard disk) and on which the register is conducted has the proprietary right of ownership to this information bearer.

It follows from this that, for the party that is not effecting the fixation of property rights in the transaction, this right has no proprietary, material expression.

When depositing securities in a bank custody account, their transition from tangible — material (on a paper medium) — into intangible — immaterial (non-cash — in the form of deeds to a custody account) — does not change the essence of the securities, their nature and their value content. Only the medium on which they are represented changes.

Property rights reflected in an obligation are not changed when the medium of the obligations changes.

At the same time, the principle of the «right from a document» is completely inapplicable to registered causal securities, as it makes absolutely no difference who has this security or whether it exists at all, because the commanding role in this instance is acquired by the entry made in the register of the party that is obliged in these legal relations, not by the record on the security.

Neither will this principle ever be applicable to non-cash, uncertificated securities, because these do not have a medium expressed for the right holder. And it is in precisely these securities that the principle of the supremacy of the register becomes exclusive.

Moreover, using the logical method of argument *a contrario*, one can logically conclude that, if the proprietary right of ownership to one's own paper copy of a contract, such as a loan, exists, then the loan is a property right, which is incorrect. (If B comes from A, and B is false, than A is false.)

Thus, using a number of methods, we have explained that **a security is not an object, but a type of contract (agreement).**

To any critics of this point of view I pose the question: what is the pivotal difference between a loan agreement (contract) and an obligation, which makes it possible to ascribe a loan agreement to the sphere of law of obligations, and an obligation to the sphere of property law?

The answer is that there is no pivotal difference, as is confirmed by Article 816 of the CC RF: «In cases provided for by law or other legal acts, **a loan agreement may be concluded by issuing or selling obligations**» (author's bold).

Part III
MONEY

Money as an economic and value category

As you will remember, Article 128 of the CC RF categorises money as objects, although the world's leading economists believe that the function of money may be fulfilled by both objects and obligations.

There follows a number of quotes.

Encyclopedia Americana:

«Money can be anything of which the use is accepted everywhere and universally for payment for goods, services and debts»[1].

Russian Legal Encyclopedia:

«MONEY — 1) in the economic sense — special goods or objects that serve as a general countervalue within the framework of commodity circulation of a specific national economy; 2) in the legal sense — items which are object of civil law and fulfil in civil turnover the function of a general instrument of counter-value to the extent that it is not prohibited by the State (M. proper), as well as items produced after models defined by law, by specialist government enterprises, and recognised by the State as the sole legal means of payment with a properly forced exchange rate in relation to M., which is expressed *in a national monetary unit (national currency) (monetary symbols)*»[2].

R. Barr:

«Money has had different forms over time and space. Its physical properties are not definitive: all kinds of money — silver and gold coins, banknotes, cheques, bank transfers — are means of payment; they do not have common physical characteristics, and some of them are not even of a material nature»[3].

---

[1] Encyclopaedia Americana. Vol. 19. 1988. P. 349.
[2] Russian Legal Encyclopedia. Moscow, 1999. P. 719–720 (Российская юридическая энциклопедия. М., 1999. С. 719–720).
[3] *R. Barr.* Political economy. Vol. 2. Moscow, 1995. P. 281.

Rist:

«Paper money acquires the capacity to retain value as a result of an act of volition»[1].

Aristotle:

«Money became money (*nomisma*) not through its internal character, but on the strength of the law (*nomos*), and it is within our power to change this situation and render it useless.»

C.R. McConnell, S.L. Brue:

«Metal and paper money are obligations of the State and agents of the State. Current accounts represent obligations of commercial banks and savings institutions»[2].

K. Marx:

«Exchange value, separated from the goods themselves and existing alongside them as an independent commodity, is money»[3];

«Money is a particular commodity which thus represents the adequate existence of the exchange value of all goods as a particular, allotted commodity[4];

«Credit money means money in the form of some kind of obligation»[5].

L.N. Krasavina, analysing Marx, elaborates:

«Money in itself is not an object but a historically defined form of economic — that is, socio-productive — relations between people in the process of commodity exchange. Money is a historically developing economic category: at each stage of goods production, it is filled with new content of a specific type of production relations, expressed through a universal cost equivalent. This content is complicated by a change in reproduction conditions and objective criteria for the formation of labour input and commodity value that are necessary for society. In the pre-capitalist stages of development, money expressed the production relations between individual goods manufacturers; under condi-

---

[1] *S. Rist.* Histoire des doctrines relatives à la monnaie et au credit. Paris, 1938.

[2] *C.R. McConnell, S.L. Brue.* Economics: principles, problems and politics. Moscow, 1992. P. 265.

[3] *K. Marx, F. Engels.* Complete works. 2nd edition. Vol. 46. Part I. P. 87.

[4] *Ibidem.* Vol. 13. P. 35.

[5] *K. Marx.* Capital. A critique of political economy. Vol. I // *K. Marx, F. Engels.* Complete works.Vol. 23. P. 151.

tions of pre-monopoly capitalism, it expressed the production relations between the goods manufacturer and society; and under monopoly capitalism, between the goods manufacturer and the world market»[1].

A.G. Gryaznova:

«Money is an economic category in which public relations are manifest, and with whose assistance public relations are conducted»[2].

O.I. Lavrushin:

«Money is an economic category in which public relations are manifest, and with whose assistance these relations are built; money acts as an independent form of exchange value, and medium of exchange, payment and hoarding»[3].

P. Berger:

«Money is issued by three kinds of institutions: commercial banks, the State Treasury and an issuing bank»[4].

L. Harris:

«Money is defined as any commodity which functions as a medium of exchange, a unit of payment and a means of retaining value»[5].

N.G. Mankiw:

«Money is the sum of assets regularly used by people to acquire goods and services from other individuals»[6].

C.J. Woelfel:

«The admissibility of concrete forms of money for the payment of debts is established by a law which defines it as a LEGAL MEANS OF PAYMENT and, consequently, allows a debtor to present it to clear his debt»[7].

---

[1] *L.N. Krasavina*. Currency and credit under capitalism. Moscow, 1989. P. 9 (*Красавина Л.Н.* Денежное обращение и кредит при капитализме. М., 1989. С. 9).

[2] *A.G. Gryaznova*. Finance and credit encyclopaedic dictionary. Moscow, 2002. P. 267 (*Грязнова А.Г.* Финансово-кредитный энциклопедический словарь. М., 2002. С. 267).

[3] *O.I. Lavrushin*. Money, credit, banks. Moscow, 1999. P. 9 (*Лаврушин О.И.* Деньги, кредит, банки. М., 1999. С. 9).

[4] *P. Berger*. The money mechanism. Moscow, 1993. P. 21.

[5] *L. Harris*. Monetary theory. Moscow: Progress, 1990. P. 75.

[6] *N.G. Mankiw*. The principles of economics. St Petersburg, 1999.

[7] *C.J. Woelfel*. Encyclopedia of banking affairs and finances. Moscow, 2000. P. 290.

Money is the greatest invention of civilisation and infiltrates all spheres of human activity. It is fundamentally more important than simply an instrument of the economic system. It is fair to say that an efficiently functional monetary system exerts a positive influence on the circulation of revenue and expenses, which is also the essence of economics. A monetary system that works well promotes more effective use of available production and human (labour) potential; it ensures full employment and prevents the growth of inflation and social tension at the same time. And on the other hand, a poorly functioning monetary system that is inadequate with regard to existing reality can cause sharp fluctuations in production levels, a recession in the economy, and various social crises.

«The essence of money lies in the fact that it serves as a necessary active component and composite part of the economic activity of society, and of the relations between different participants in the reproduction and distribution process»[1]. Money is a constituent of commodity relations. The advent and development of goods brings with it the advent and development of money. This inseparable pair — goods and money — is a perpetual form of movement in economic life.

«Money 'underwent' a protracted evolutionary process and under the influence of the progress of civilisation radically changed its form, character, content and essence.

The most important factors in the transformation of money were the development and growing complexity:

firstly, of productive forces;

secondly, of production relations, including trade-money relations, and credit relations as a part of the latter. Money, as is widely known, is a part of trade-money relations;

thirdly, of the superstructure: the State and the laws which are created by the State.

So, that which gave rise to this phenomenon of human society, by developing and becoming more and more complex, led money to a similar result»[2].

---

[1] *A.G. Gryaznova.* Aforementioned work. P. 267.
[2] *M.P. Berezina.* Credit money: Academic essay for practical use // *Business and banks,* 2003. Issue 21–22 (*Березина М.П.* Кредитные деньги: Научное эссе с пользой для практики // *Бизнес и банки,* 2003. № 21–22).

The commodity origin of money

Many schools of theory link the question of the origin of money with the development process of the exchange of goods.

For any product to become a commodity, it had to:

- be produced not for personal use, but for sale;
- satisfy certain requirements, i.e. have utility value. Moreover, the commodity must be useful to the purchaser, a fact that is confirmed by the sale and purchase of the commodity;
- have value. The value of a commodity consists of any costs associated with it, and moreover, not the individual costs of the manufacturer (cost price), but costs recognised by the public. This must also be acknowledged by purchase and sale.

Only the sum of these three conditions makes a product a commodity. The absence of any of these means that the product is not a commodity. For example, if a certain product is produced for personal use or it is impossible to buy or sell it, then this product is not a commodity.

The exchange of individual products of social labour between primitive communities had an incidental character. The development of commodity exchange was linked with the first large-scale social division of labour — between cattle-breeding and agricultural tribes. The second large-scale division of labour — the separation of crafts from agriculture — led to commodity production and regular exchange between private owners.

A. Smith wrote: «... Any rational person, at any level of the development of society after the division of labour, had to organise his business so that he permanently had a certain amount of the type of commodity which he was sure that nobody would refuse to accept in exchange for products of his trade»[1].

As a result of the development of commodity exchange, a particular commodity stood out, which had the greatest sale capacity — money, having divided the process of the mutual exchange of commodities (C — C) into two simultaneously functioning processes: sale (C — M) and acquisition (M — C). This made it possible to overcome individu-

---

[1] Quoted from: *E.F. Borisov.* Economic theory: reading book. Moscow, 2000. P. 20 (*Борисов Е.Ф.* Экономическая теория: Хрестоматия. М., 2000. С. 20).

al, quantitative, time and space constraints that are characteristic of trade, and thus to significantly reduce transaction expenses of exchange.

Functions

Every phenomenon, in order to display its existence and characteristics, must show its worth in practice. «The economic essence of money manifests itself in its functions»[1], and modern economic literature draws the concept of money from the functions it fulfils. «Anything that fulfils the functions of money is money»[2]. Thus, anything which people accept as money and which fulfils the functions of money can be used as money.

According to Marx, money fulfils five functions:

1) a measure of value;

2) a medium of exchange;

3) a means of payment (all spheres of commodity circulation);

4) a store of value;

5) universal money[3].

Many Western academics recognise just three functions of money:

1) a medium of exchange (payment);

2) a measure of value;

3) a means of hoarding and saving (retaining value)[4].

However, they all agree that anything which people recognise as money and which fulfils the functions of money can be used as money.

Generally speaking, in economic theory there is no single opinion on the functions of money. The point of view of Professor Yu. I. Kashin is worthy of attention; he suggests that universal money is not an independent function, but just a spatially limited area of its use. Equally interesting is his evaluation of the transformation of such function as «a means of hoarding and saving» into the function of «reposing money», guaranteeing credit-issuing circulation through its presence in any

---

[1] *O.I. Lavrushin*. Aforementioned work. P. 13.
[2] *C.R. McConnell, S. L. Brue*. Economics. P. 264.
[3] See: *K. Marx*. Capital. A critique of the political economy. Vol. I // *K. Marx, F. Engels*. Complete works. Vol. 23. P. 118–151.
[4] See: *P. Samuelson*. Economics. Vol. I. Moscow, 1992. P. 258; *A.J. Dolan, C.D. Campbell, R.J. Campbell*. Money, banking affairs and monetary and credit policy. Moscow-Leningrad, 1991. P. 30–34; *P. Berger*. The money mechanism. Moscow, 1993. P. 13–15.

depository[1]. From time to time, money is given a secondary function — an ideological-proclamatory function. This played a significant role after the Battle of Kulikovo (when Russia won a decisive victory over the Mongol opressors), and also when Russia was liberated from the Poles (uprising of Minin and Pozharsky), as well as from 1917 to 1924.

The functions of money are regarded as a manifestation of its essence. Furthermore, these functions are fulfilled only with the participation of people who can separate the value of goods from their user and exchange value, who accept money in the process of commodity exchange and other payments, and also use it as a means of hoarding. This means that money is an instrument of economic relations in society, but **the functions of money can only be fulfilled with people's participation.**

Within the framework of this study, we are primarily interested in the economic function of circulation and payment, and the legal rules of monetary circulation.

As a means of payment, money is used for payments outside the sphere of commodity exchange. A particular characteristic of this function of money is a time interval between the movement of money and the movement of goods and services: for example, taxes, welfare payments, interest on credit. Money is easily accepted as a means of payment. This is a convenient social invention, which makes it possible to pay owners of resources and producers of «goods» (with money), and which may be used to purchase any of a wide selection of goods and services available on the market.

As currency, money functions within the sphere of commodity exchange. Today, money is a medium of exchange first and foremost, and can be used to buy and sell goods and services.

As a medium of exchange, money enables society to avoid the inconveniences of barter exchange. Representing a convenient way of exchanging goods, money allows society to make use of the products of geographical specialisation and the division of labour between people.

---

[1] See: *Yu.I. Kashin.* On the subject of modifying the functions of money // *Money and credit,* 2002. Issue. 1. P. 64–66 (*Кашин Ю.И.* К вопросу о модификации функций денег // *Деньги и кредит,* 2002. № 1. С. 64–66).

It is important to note that business entities choose the form of money that most precisely corresponds to the requirements before them: if they need to buy a newspaper, they will get small change ready; if a legal person is expecting to have to pay taxes, then he will have ready in advance the required amount of non-cash money in his bank account. If payments are maintained over time, or if there is no specific deadline for a potential payment, the business entity will try to choose the form of conserving value which would, firstly, have the necessary liquidity, and secondly, yield a certain revenue over time. Conservation of value in the form of money can lead to «lost profit expenses». In order to avoid this, every business environment nowadays has the optimum balance between liquidity, profitability and risk capital. However, as a rule, other resources, such as bank deposits and revenue securities of companies, banks and the State are also used.

Properties

Money must have the following properties:

* liquidity;
* portability;
* durability;
* divisibility;
* standardisability;
* recognisability.

The most important of these properties in money is liquidity. Absolute liquidity means that an owner of money, using this money, can at any time fulfil any financial obligation, because money can always be used a legal tender. The most important requirement for conforming to this characteristic is for money to receive general (and, ideally, governmental) recognition, both from purchasers and vendors, as a medium of exchange.

Settlement of commodity conflicts using money

Based on the study of factual material, Karl Marx scientifically proved that money is a historical category that is inherent in goods production. But in order to understand the origin and commercial nature of money, and to explain how and why money made its mark in the world of trade, let us look first of all at commodity conflicts and ways of resolving it. Modern economic theory identifies the following

basic commodity conflicts that have arisen through exchange and have been resolved with money as a universal cost equivalent between:
- consumer and exchange value;
- concrete and abstract labour (between subjective and objective utility);
- the private and public nature of labour.

Money according to its own underlying essence is exchange value separated from a commodity, used in everyday economic practice.

Commodity — unity of consumer and exchange value; and *value* is the unity of the utility of a commodity and the cost of producing it. Value is the material form of the cost of abstract public labour, expressing the relationship between the vendor and the purchaser, or between cost and profitability.

Consumer value — the ability of a commodity to meet this or that requirement of a person; its usefulness.

Exchange value — the ability of a commodity to be exchanged in specified quantitative proportions for another commodity.

«Objects which have a very high consumer value often have an extremely low exchange value or even none at all; in contrast, objects which have a very high exchange value often have a very low consumer value or none at all. There is nothing more useful than water, yet one can buy nothing with it. On the other hand, a diamond has almost no consumer value, but in exchange for it one can receive a very large quantity of goods»[1].

Money as a measure of value and as a medium of exchange forms a union of opposites. One function presupposes the other, as the use of money ensures the movement of value and consumer value. On this basis, Karl Marx developed the methodological principle: «... a commodity turns into money primarily as the unity of a measure of value and a medium of exchange...»[2].

In the union of the functions of a measure of value and a medium of exchange, their contrast and contradiction become apparent. Firstly, as a measure of value, money acts as ideal money, and in the function

---

[1] Quoted from: *E. F. Borisov.* Aforementioned work. P. 22.
[2] See: *K. Marx.* Capital. A critique of the political economy. Vol. I // *K. Marx, F. Engels.* Complete works. Vol. 23.

of a medium of exchange, it acts as real money. Secondly, the function of a measure of value is fulfilled by full-bodied money, while in the function of a medium of exchange, it is replaced by tokens of value.

To quote Karl Marx: «As a result of the first process of turnover, sale, emerges the initial point of the second process, money. Goods in their initial form were replaced by their equivalent in gold. This result may, first of all, suspend the process, as a commodity in this second form has a natural existence capable of waiting. A commodity in the hands of its owner has no consumer value, when it is available in a form that is always fit for use, as it is always in a position to be exchanged, and it only depends on the obligations when and at what point on the surface of the world of trade it enters into circulation again. The presence of a commodity in the form of a gold chrysalis forms an independent period in its life, in which it can remain more or less for an extended period of time»[1].

When a commodity enters the market, that is, into the sphere of exchange, this contradiction appears as a conflict between the consumer value and the exchange value, or between the private and the public profitability of a commodity. This conflict is solved by dividing the commodity into two: the commodity and money.

The solution of this contradiction in a commodity is the exchange operation of a commodity for money, during which the user value of the commodity is definitively separated from its value. Thus the market solves the problem of providing for the public in the person of purchasers with goods that it needs, while the producers of these goods are rewarded with corresponding income.

Thus, the necessity of money is caused by the conflict between exchange value and consumer value within a commodity. The contrast between these two categories of values, which are linked with each other, occurs in the debates of all classical economists on the subject of the theory of prices. For A. Smith, this contrast is between consumer value and exchange value, while for the founders of the marginal utility theory it is the contrast between subjective and objective utility.

These two sides of value represent the union of opposites. The union of consumer value and exchange value is defined by the fact that these are comparable values. Exchange value is a certain quantity of con-

---

[1] Ibidem.

sumer value, measured on a universal scale accepted for this purpose by society.

In our opinion, Russian economist M. A. Portnoy described very well the reason for the origin of money under the conditions of commodity production:

«And so, every commodity, i.e. product, that is created to be sold, bears within itself a contradiction as the object of public economic relations, acting as the unity and conflict of opposites, and is expressed as a range of interlinked and mutually conditional contradictions between:

• the individual and society;
• consumer value (utility) and value (social utility);
• presence and essence;
• private and general (public).

These conflicts cannot be solved by themselves. To solve them, the commodity in question must be confronted with its opposite, whose role was fulfilled, at the more primitive stage of trade, by another commodity, and at more developed stage, by money. The commodity conflict is solved by exchange — a buy-sell transaction — in which the vendor — the owner of the commodity — participates on the one hand, and the purchaser — the owner of equivalent value — on the other. At the same time the vendor acts as a separate individual, personifying the private principle, and the purchaser represents the public, embodying public interest. The exchange is an act of public recognition of the useful quality of the productive activity of a particular individual (or enterprise), and at the same time solves the conflict between the individual and the public, and all subsequent conflicts.

Since the purchaser represents the public in this act, the purchase of the commodity means that the public as a body has approved the productive activity of the individual who is the owner and seller of this commodity.

As a result of the exchange, the consumer value (utility) of the commodity is separated from its value (public utility).

With the development of trade and the appearance of money, the world of trade split into two poles: at one pole are all the goods that embody the current consumer value (utility); and at the other is the money which embodies value (public utility).

All goods are now becoming varieties of one or the other phenomenon. They all represent utilities designed to meet various needs, when their universal essence is expressed henceforth in money. Goods are now products with a corresponding purpose, while money is the embodiment and measure of their value.

Goods, having been traded, are transformed from their potential value into real value. Before they had been sold, they were products of private economic activity, the expediency of which remained under question. After the buy-sell transaction, the commodity becomes a component of public wealth, expressed in money. Private energies expended on creating it are recognised as an adequate proportion of public energies, the scale of which is represented in monetary form.

Thus, money is:

- *the embodiment of value, the personification of public utility;*
- *the essence of goods as values, their universal characteristic as components of public wealth»*[1].

It would be hard to exaggerate the significance of money as a medium of exchange, as it allows one to avoid the barter form of trade. The replacement of barter exchange by monetary exchange separates the act of sale from the act of purchase. If money exists, the vendor of a commodity only has to find someone who wants to buy his commodity, and having received the money, he can buy anything he wants. The replacement of the bartering method of transactions with a system that uses money as a medium of exchange leads to a reduction in turnover expenses. Far less time and energy is needed for monetary exchange than for barter. By lowering turnover expenses, money stimulated the development of specialisation and trade.

Let us sum up the significance of money's function as a medium of exchange. As such, money:

- mediates the movement of goods and services, facilitating their circulation process;
- overcomes constraints of quantity, time and space characteristic of barter exchange;
- reduces turnover expenses.

---

[1] *M.A. Portnoy.* Money, its forms and functions. Moscow, 1998. P. 22–23 (*Портной М.А.* Деньги, их виды и функции. М., 1998. С. 22–23).

Money, which arose naturally from the need to resolve commodity conflicts, nevertheless became more than simply a subject of heightened interest for the administrative systems of governments. Governments began to impose means of payment that were controlled by the State (currency) on controlled economies, and through legislation to limit the circulation of other methods of payment; and, as a result, the only legal monetary resource left was the currency of that particular government.

Both the monetarist and the Keynesian theories directly advocate the regulation of forms of money, money supply and interest rates in order to influence the economy.

Thus, the money which arose in an evolutionary way from economic relations was gradually ousted by the State and replaced with money that arose through law and legislation. It is only in times of economic crises, when the State proves unable to properly support the function of the national currency as money, that the economy falls back on the use of full-bodied, commodity money or barter.

In this way, the ambivalence of the basis and superstructure, of the economy and legislation, is revealed in the change in the nature and essence of money.

The role of money is characterised by the results of its use and its influence on various aspects of the activity and development of society.

The role of money is most evident in the results of its part in the establishment of commodity prices. The role of money changes as conditions of economic development change. Its role increases with a shift to a market economy.

The concept of «money» is interpreted differently in Russian legal practice, than in the country's economic practice. Article 140 of the CC RF is entitled «Money (currency)» and states: «The rouble is the legal means of payment and is to be accepted by nominal cost throughout the territory of the Russian Federation». Thereby, the legal definition of the word «money» is the same as the economic meaning of «currency» and is considered to be **«the monetary unit of a particular government, established by law»**[1].

[1] *L.N. Krasavina.* International currency-credit and financial relations. Moscow, 2000. P. 34 (*Красавина Л.Н.* Международные валютно-кредитные и финансовые отношения. М., 2000. С. 34).

However, it will be demonstrated in this study that the concept of «currency» does not include commodity or financial money, and is only a subset of the concept of «credit money»; and, of course, is essentially a subset of the concept of «money».

So as to avoid confusion, we shall use the economic meaning of the word «money».

Money supply

Neither among economists, nor among government officials, is there a consensus of opinion on the question of which separate elements make up monetary supply in the economy. It is extremely difficult to draw a line between money proper and other liquid assets which partially fulfil the functions of money. Only local currency has absolute liquidity as a method of payment that has to be accepted — which is provided for by public law. Other liquid assets are a means of payment only in the event that the beneficiary agrees to accept them, i.e. a transaction exists on the basis of civil law. However, one should remember that a certain proportion of payment transactions and commodity turnover is served by liquid assets, which are gladly accepted by beneficiaries, but whose circulation is prohibited in a country on the basis of public law — for example, the US dollar in Russia[1]. In Russia it is also forbidden to circulate bars of precious metals and materials which contain them, as well as precious stones and rare-earth metals[2].

In a narrow sense, the supply of money, known as M0, consists of cash, that is, metal and paper money which is in circulation. M1, according to C. R. McConnell and S. L. Brue[3], comprises M0 and checkable deposits, i.e. deposits in commercial banks, different savings banks or savings establishments, for which cheques can be written[4]. In Russia, checkable deposits are not as widespread as in other western countries.

Western economists also distinguish «quasi-money» — aggregates M2 and M3. «Quasi-money» are certain highly-liquid financial assets

---

[1] This is with the exception of operations of subjects with banks that have an appropriate license.

[2] See Federal Law No. 3615-1 «On currency regulation and currency control», dated 9 October 1992.

[3] *C.R. McConnell, S. L. Brue*. Economics. Moscow, 1992. Vol. 1. P. 264.

[4] On the condition that local vendors everywhere accept cheques as a means of payment for goods and services both for retail and wholesale transactions. (*Author's note*).

such as chequeless savings accounts, deposit accounts and short-term government securities, which do not function directly as a method of payment, but may easily and without risk of financial losses be changed into cash or cheque accounts. In contrast, for example, with the USA, in Russia deposit accounts may be closed by the depositor and, before the expiry of the deadline, without payment of a fine.

M2 includes elements of the medium of exchange (cash and checkable deposits), in accordance with M1, and other elements, which may be converted quickly and without loss into cash and checkable deposits.

The third, «official» definition of M3 in the USA is based on the fact that large (100,000 dollars or more) deposit accounts, which enterprises usually own in the form of certificates of deposit, are also easily converted into checkable deposits. An active market for such certificates does, in fact, exist, and so it is possible to sell (liquidate) them at any time, albeit with a possible risk of loss (in Russia an example of this is presented by the loan bonds of different tranches, which are sold with a significant reduction from their nominal value, if the deadline for redeeming them expires in 5–6 years or more).

To calculate the total money supply in the Russian Federation, provision is made for the following aggregates:

*   M0 — cash money;
*   M1 = M0 plus operating accounts and demand accounts;
*   M2 = M1 plus deposit accounts;
*   M3 = M2 plus certificates of deposit and State loan bonds.

There is a whole range of assets (they differ from country to country, but a certain similarity is apparent), which differ only slightly from each other by degree of liquidity or availability of monetary funds.

Which of the definitions of money listed above is preferable? Most western and Russian economists choose M1. Why? This simple definition includes everything that is directly used as a medium of exchange.

The evolution of money forms

The functions of money in their evolutionary process were fulfilled, and continue to be fulfilled, by both objects and obligations.

Money has different forms over time and space. The form of money in the economic sense must be understood to mean the type of material goods which fulfils the function of money at the appropriate level of economic and legal development of society (Fig. 6).

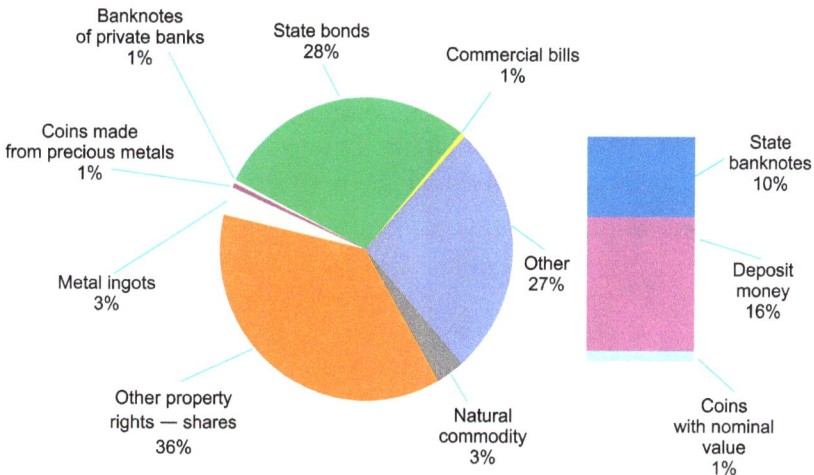

Fig. 6. Ratio of different forms of money in circulation

The prevalence of and demand for one form of money or another is defined by indicators such as negotiability, convenience, portability, durability, divisibility, demand, and sufficient amount in circulation.

It is necessary to point out the following basic forms of money which arose in the process of evolution:

1) *natural money*:

a) non-standardised goods including metals by weight (commercial metals);

b) precise-weight metal ingots;

2) *credit money*:

a) commercial bills;

b) banknotes of private banks;

c) currency:
- cash currency:
  - state banknotes (treasury notes) backed by metal;
  - state banknotes (treasury notes) not backed by metal;
  - coins with nominal value;
- non-cash money — deposit money (checkable accounts);
  3) *financial money*:
  a) quasi-money;
  b) stock which fulfils the function of money to a limited extent.

These forms sprang up successively, as a rule, and were prevalent in certain periods of time (Table 3). New forms of money arose primarily because it was necessary to minimise trading costs and to accelerate accounting and trade operations (Fig. 7).

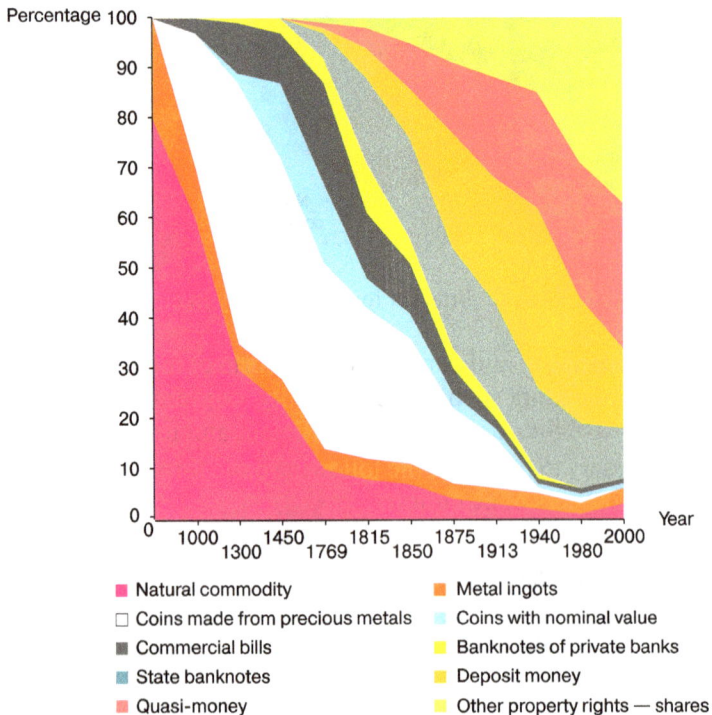

Fig. 7. The ousting of old forms of money by new forms of money

Table 3

Share of different forms of money at different times, %

Money	0	1000	1300	1450	1769	1815	1850	1875	1913	1940	1980	2000
Natural commodity	80	60	30	23	10	8	7	4	3	2	1	3
Metal ingots	20	10	5	5	4	4	4	3	3	3	2	3
Coins made from precious metals	0	27	52	44	37	30	25	15	10	1	1	0
Commercial bills	0	3	10	10	20	13	10	5	2	1	1	1
Banknotes of private banks	0	0	1	3	5	10	5	4	3	1	0	0
State banknotes	0	0	0	0	5	17	20	20	20	17	13	10
Coins with nominal value	0	0	2	15	16	6	5	3	2	1	1	1
Deposit money	0	0	0	0	1	6	10	23	25	36	25	16
Quasi-money	0	0	0	0	1	4	9	14	20	23	27	29
Other property rights — shares	0	0	0	0	1	2	5	9	12	15	29	37

In his work «Money: its forms and functions», M. A. Portnoy categorises the fundamental historical phases of commodity money relations (Table 4)[1].

Table 4

Schematic classification of the basic historical stages of commodity-money relations

Key commodities	Money
1. Natural exchange	
Products	Products (livestock, fur, fish, etc., metals and, finally, silver and gold)
2. Regular trade	
Products	Gold and silver
3. Capitalist production of the free competition era	
Products (consumer and investment goods); land; workforce (labour); monetary capital	Gold and silver; credit money (commercial bills, banknotes, deposit money)
4. Modern capitalism	
Products (consumer and investment goods); land; workforce (labour); business; monetary capital	Credit and financial money (commercial bills, banknotes, deposit money, bonds, shares and other securities)

They all have the right to exist even today, and only public (or State) recognition can force one kind of material goods or another out of circulation or confer on it the status of legal money.

Looking at these forms of money in consecutive order, we shall try to define their properties as objects and as obligations.

[1] *M.A. Portnoy.* Money: its forms and functions. Moscow: Ankil, 1998. P. 7 (*Портной А.М.* Деньги: их виды и функции. М.: Анкил, 1998. С. 7).

Natural money

Natural commodity money

Percentage

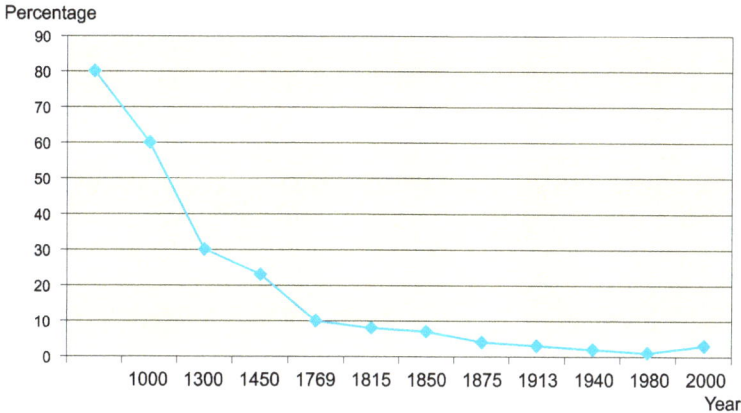

Fig. 8. Prevalence of natural commodity money

When certain goods or services are directly exchanged for others, it immediately becomes apparent that some goods are needed for a wider range of purchasers than other goods, and this gives rise to public acceptance of them as forms of money (Fig. 8).

If we look at the evolution of money in the early stages of the development of society and public relations, we discover that at that time, it was mainly natural commodity money that was in demand:

* kauri shells (Polynesia, India);
* squirrel and sable pelts, slate spindle whorls — weights used in spinning[1] (Ancient Russia);
* bricks of natural salt (Ethiopia)[2];
* iron hoes (Sudan)[3];
* beaded belts — wampums (South American Indians);
* bottles of vodka and tins of stew — in remote regions of Russia during so-called developed socialism (1970–1980s);

---

[1] *A.S. Melnikova.* Money of Russia. 1000 years. Moscow, 2000. P. 18 (*Мельникова А.С.* Деньги России. 1000 лет. М., 2000. С. 18).
[2] *J. Cribb.* Money. Dorling Kindersley, 1999. P. 8.
[3] *Ibidem.*

- copper and bronze (Ancient Rome);
- iron (Sparta)[1].

Among nomads, cattle played the role of money; among landowners, cultivated vegetable crops; among hunters, animal pelts[2].

In Ancient Rome and Ancient Greece, wealth was measured by the number of cattle, and herds were driven to market with which to pay for anticipated purchases. Homer judged the worth of Achilles' shield and armour in oxen: in Latin, the word *pecunia* (money) is derived from the word *pecus* (herd). It is interesting that the Latin root of the word «capital» comes from *capital*, meaning cattle. In Russian, exchangeable counterparts were called kuna — from the skin of the marten (kunit-sa).

«Pelts of valuable furry animals fulfilled the function of «fur» money. The units of value of these goods that were equivalent to money were «kuna» (marten pelts) and bela (squirrel (belka) pelts). In a Smolensk document dating from 1150, a fox pelt was valued at 12 kuna. Various kinds of levies (yasak) were paid into public coffers in leather pelts. Pelts were a common form of money for ancient states — Sparta, Rome, Carthage. Chronicles of Scandinavian peoples recount how on land where animals were to be found in abundance, pelts were used as money, to pay for purchases and to pay taxes and fines. In the code of laws of the time, it was stated that for an insult, the offender must pay one fox pelt, for physical mutilation a sable pelt, and so on. [...] «Fur» and «leather» money were still in circulation during the reign of Peter the Great. And until very recently, pelts were used as money in Alaska.

When metal money was first used in Ancient Russia it was called «kuna» (the price of a marten pelt) or «bela» (the price of a squirrel pelt), and only with the passage of time did these old names gradually die out»[3].

«Also, rice was used in Japan, tea in China, cotton cloths in Africa and dried fish in Iceland. For example, prices in Iceland in the 15th century were as follows:

for a horseshoe — 1 dried fish;

---

[1] *R. Barr.* Aforementioned work. P. 283.
[2] *L.V. Orlenko.* The history of trade. Moscow, 2006. P. 58 (*Орленко Л.В.* История торговли. М., 2006. С. 58).
[3] *Ibidem.* P. 59.

for a pair of women's shoes — 3 fishes;
for a keg of wine — 100 fishes;
for a keg of butter — 120 fishes.

Natural money, being of material value itself, was most suitable in the role of money at this time, when commodity production was as yet insufficiently developed and had not become the basic form of public production. The necessity of using natural money was the result of the disunity, the insulation of individual goods manufacturers, for whom only the exchange of products acted as a way to connect economically and socially, confirming the utility of their product and compensating the owners of the goods for the value of that product in the form of equivalent material valuables»[1].

It is worth noting that society, during severe economic crises and upsets, losing faith in the possibility of other, higher forms fulfilling the function of money, lowers itself to this form of commodity circulation, bashfully calling it barter.

For example, in Russia at the end of 1991, during a period of economic reforms, the deficit in goods became so severe that money ceased to be of any use — all trade began to take place on the basis of barter. And there and then, «monetary» commodities appeared (automobiles, timber, steel, petrol, meat), in exchange for which you could receive anything you needed. For example, for a tonne of petrol you could get 4.2 tonnes of cement, 70kg of meat, or 1100 red bricks.

Some economists call this the commodity-accounting phase.

This is how Professor N. G. Mankiw of Harvard University describes the situation in his book, «The Principles of Economics»:

«**In cases when a commodity takes over the role of money, having intrinsic value, it is called commodity money.** The concept of **intrinsic** value is applied to money which will still have value when it is not being used as money. A well-known example of commodity money is gold, which has intrinsic value because it is used both in industry and to manufacture jewellery... Another example of commodity money is cigarettes. During the Second World War, prisoners in PoW camps sold various goods and services to each

---

[1] *M.A. Portnoy.* Money: its forms and functions. P. 32 (*Портной М.А.* Деньги: их виды и функции. С. 32).

other using cigarettes as a means of hoarding, a unit of accounting and a medium of exchange. In this situation, even non-smokers gladly accepted cigarettes as payment, as they knew that they could always use them to obtain other goods and services»[1].

Circulation

Natural money, having served individual and small wholesale irregular turnover, circulates in accordance with the simplest property rules: whoever has the article in his hands is the owner. The simple transfer of the article from the hands of one to another constituted the simplest exchange. As a rule, no contractual relations encroached upon the exchange.

As the variety of goods on the market increased, the problem experienced by vendors and purchasers of determining the dominant commodity in circulation became ever more pressing.

In an evolutionary process, metal began to force other goods out of circulation because it had the greatest capacity to be used in the economy not only as an instrument of circulation but also (after treatment) as tools of labour or weapons: a plough, pitcher, knife, sword, shield or other, similar goods could be transformed more easily than other commodities into no less valuable items, which meant that exchange value could be converted into consumer value almost immediately after the exchange process.

Precise-weight metal ingots

As regular trade developed, and particularly as the volume of wholesale transactions grew to several carriages or wagons of goods such as expensive fabrics and high-quality metal wares, and as industrial relations reached the stage of contracts for the construction of palaces and fortresses, society started to consider gold to be the universal equivalent (Fig. 9). As Cantillon writes, «gold and silver, and only they, are small in size (with high value — A. G.), of equally high quality, easy to transport, do not produce by-products when they are exchanged, are easy to store, the objects which can be produced from them are beautiful and brilliant, and they can be used infinitely»[2].

---

[1] *N.G. Mankiw.* The Principles of Economics. St. Petersburg, 1999. P. 589.
[2] Quotation from: *R. Barr.* Political economy. Vol. 2. Moscow, 1995. P. 283.

Percentage

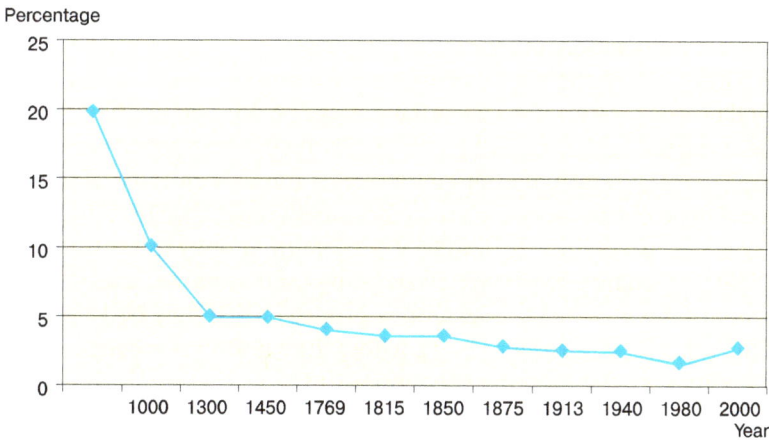

Fig. 9. Prevalence of precise-weight metal ingots

In other words, this commodity ensured a simple transaction and reduced transaction expenses.

Gold bars used as money were circulated in the form of a standard geometric mass of uniform shape, composition and weight, which was certified by a special stamp on the bar. The production and branding of these bars, naturally, was the prerogative of the highest authorities, that is, sovereigns and high priests. This attests to the fact that they were sufficiently widely exchanged even in long-distant historical times, and that eventually exchange developed into regular trade, which dictated the need for a standard monetary equivalent certified by the higher authorities.

Such ingots were in circulation in Ancient Babylon between 3000 and 2000 B.C. Small bars of solid-weight gold (about 14g) with the Pharaoh's stamp were in circulation in Egypt around 3000 B. C.; bars without a stamp were worth less, as few people were able to distinguish gold from a counterfeit, but they trusted the stamp of the Pharaoh. Only expert craftsmen and masters of the gold industry could forge the Pharaoh's stamp at that level of technological development, and each of these men was well-known. Also, the punishment for such forgery was extremely severe.

It is worth noting that **the first promissory component appeared in this money and, even then, the first demand appeared not for consumer value, but for exchange value.**

The exchange value in the gold bars was the ruler's legal guarantee of their composition and weight. «In situations when one could only be certain of the authenticity of metal currency by means of a complicated testing process, for which the average person was neither qualified nor equipped, the stamp of a universally recognised government body could serve as a convincing guarantee of the authenticity of the currency... The challenge, which the government took upon itself to answer, initially consisted not so much of producing money as certifying the weight and quality of the materials being used as money everywhere... Pieces of metal were seen as money proper only if they had the stamp of the relevant government body, whose duty it was, as indeed it should be, to attest to the fact that the money did in fact weigh the prescribed amount and contain metal of the proper standard, which is what gave it its value»[1].

«The names of some modern currencies hark back to when they were gold money of precise weight. For example, the English pound sterling used to be equal in England to one pound of pure silver, in William the Conqueror's time. In this form it was not minted, but acted as accounting money. The pound sterling was divided into twenty parts — shillings, each of which, in turn, was divided into twelve pence, or pennies. It is the penny, in fact, that was minted and in those times was the largest coin (K. Marx). However, in the 13th century, the weight of the English penny was equal to the weight of 32 wheat grains, «rounded, dried and taken from the middle of the ear»[2].

In 14th century Russia, bars of silver in the form of rounded batons with deep diametrical grooves, weighing up to 200g (Lithuania), or batons of triangular cross section weighing 197–200g (Novgorod), or elongated hexagons weighing about 160g (Kiev), having been given the name «grivna», were designed mostly for large accounts and payments. They were used to pay for important trade transactions, indemnities and monetary investments in monasteries, and to purchase large landed estates.

Novgorod grivnas that were split in half acquired the name «poltina» («half»)[3]. Russian precise-weight ingots had no stamp or, therefore,

---

[1] *F.A. Hayek.* Private money. Tver, 1996. P. 49.
[2] *M.A. Portnoy.* Aforementioned work. P. 59.
[3] *A.S. Melnikova.* Aforementioned work. P. 45.

promissory component, which signifies an extremely low level of development[1].

Circulation

The consumer value of such an entity was equal to the value of the metal, while the exchange value exceeded it on the scale of the value of the guarantee marked on the stamped area.

In such ingots, a promissory/liability component appeared in addition to the object component, and this was defined by the dual nature of this material commodity in the prevalence of the object component. However, the significance of the promissory component (the Pharaoh's guarantee of the composition and weight of the ingot), provided for by the property of the ruler, his right to collect taxes, to lead aggressive wars and carry out raids, made owners think about whether it was efficient to remelt ingots — for then the promissory component was lost forever, which entailed a significant loss of value.

However, the rules of circulation were carried over from the previous form of money — natural commodity money. Simple exchange functioned within the framework of property law, and the promissory component was only a part, a property of the whole entity.

Full-bodied metal coins

Gold, silver and copper coins were undoubtedly objects and had permanent value, like the value of the metal they contained. The value, for example, of the gold used to stamp gold coins was in no way dependent on the problems of the government that stamped them (Fig. 10).

The first known coins were made in the kingdom of Lydia (on the territory of present-day Turkey) in the 7th century B.C. out of electrum, a natural alloy of gold and silver. A particular design was stamped on them to confirm the prescribed weight. The minted design played the part of a stamp by which the ruler guaranteed the accuracy of the composition and weight of the coin[2].

---

[1] At this time in Russia, so-called «drogichinskiye» stamps became the promissory component of commodity money. These were lead stamps on rubbed pelts. (see: *A.S. Melnikova,* aforementioned work, P. 18).

[2] *J. Cribb.* Aforementioned work. P. 10.

Percentage

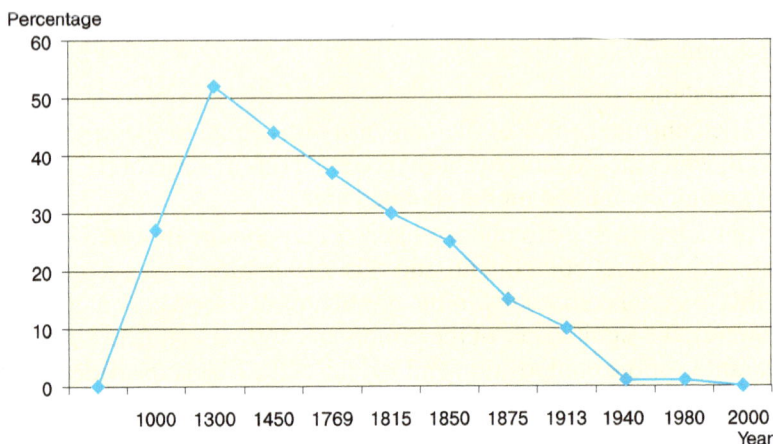

Fig. 10. Prevalence of full-bodied metal coins

On the territory of Rus', the minting of silver and gold coins dates back to the times of Prince Vladimir I (Kievan Rus, end of the 10th — beginning of the 11th century). On some gold coins, the inscription «Vladimir on the throne» was continued on the reverse with «and behold his gold», and this signified the guarantee of the coin's composition. In the «Russkaya Pravda» code of laws, metal money was still called kuna, although silver grivnas have also appeared by then. Between the 12th and the 15th centuries, princes tried to mint their own «specific» coins. In Novgorod, foreign money was in circulation — «yefimki» (from Joachimsthaler — German silver coins which were being used as an international means of payment in the whole of Eastern Europe). In the Moscow principality, the initiative to mint silver coins was taken by Dmitri Donskoi (14th century), who began to smelt Tatar silver money into Russian grivnas. Ivan III (end of the 15th century) established that the right to mint coins could belong only to the «elder» of the princes, the occupier of the Moscow throne. The first regulation of the Russian monetary system was passed under Ivan the Terrible. At the beginning of his reign, «moskovkas» and «novgorodkas» were circulating freely, and the former, at face vale, was equal to half a «novgorodka». At the beginning of the 17th century, a single monetary unit was established in Russia — the kopeck (a horseman with a spear [*kop'ye* in Russian]was depicted on the coin), which weighed 0.68g of silver. This roughly corresponded with the weight of a «novgorodka»; «moskovkas» were still being minted, as were half-kopecks and the «polushka» — a quarter of a kopeck. In addition, the rouble, the poltina and the altyn were introduced to the counting system, although the minting of the silver rouble did not become the rule until Peter the Great's reign. Gold money — the chervonets — appeared in Russia from 1718 onwards.

The growing role of the State as a body of enforcement in money circulation was demonstrated by the fact that «the population was notified before new money and polushkas were issued. In populous places, documents were hung up with the text of the tsar's decree on the new money. This decree was read out after worship in churches, and «hailed» by town criers at the markets for several days»[1].

«Nowadays we do not use gold coins, but they were circulated at markets over several centuries. The particular popularity of gold as money is due to the fact that it is relatively simple to carry, it is easy to measure, and it is possible to check it for the presence of impurities. When gold coins are used as money in the economy (or paper money, which can be exchanged for gold on demand), we say that the *gold standard* is operating in the economy»[2].

As a further example we can use the words stamped on «Nikolai's» gold coins, worth 25 roubles: «7 zolotniks 3 dolias of pure gold». [*Translator's note*: zolotnik — old Russian measure of weight equivalent to 4.26g; dolia — measure of weight equivalent to 44mg.]

The circulation of this form of money, its proprietary and promissory content, its user value and exchange value, its legal nature and security, were the same as that of precise-weight metal ingots.

---

[1] *L.V. Orlenko*. The history of trade. Moscow. 2006. P. 217 (*Орленко Л.В.* История торговли. М., 2006. С. 217).
[2] *N.G. Mankiw*. Aforementioned work. P. 589.

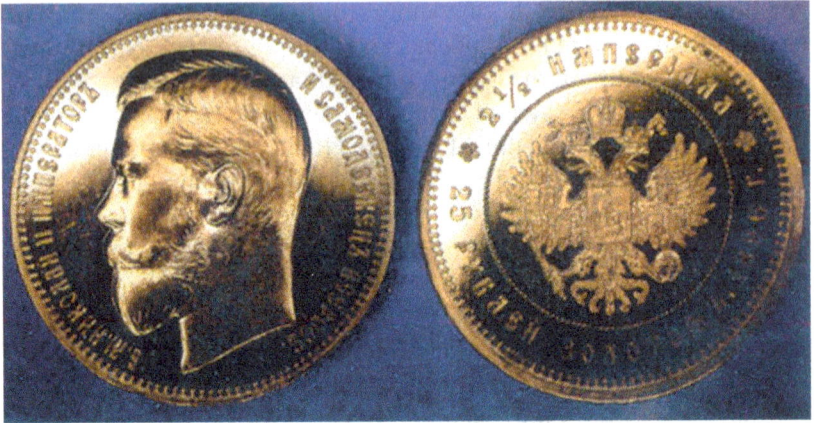

Nikolai 2nd, Emperor and Ruler
of All Russia

25 roubles of gold,
$2^1/_2$ Imperial units.
1896

25 roubles, of pure gold
3 zolotniks[1]

---

[1]   Old Russian measure of weight, equivalent to 4.26 g

Credit money

Commercial bills

Percentage

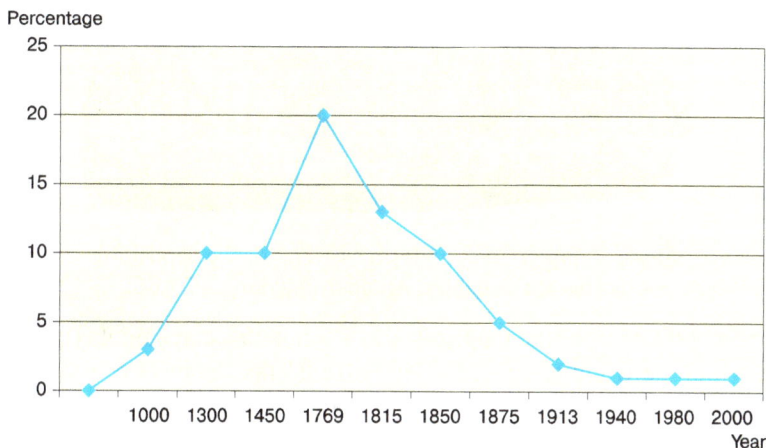

Fig. 11. Prevalence of commercial bills

The first commercial bills of exchange presently known were notes written on stone tablets for safekeeping of valuables, in use in Babylon in 3000 BC (see next page). «Gold and valuables were kept on shelves in bankers' depositories or immured into the walls (an early form of modern banking safes). For this service, Babylonian banks took 1/60th of the value of the goods deposited. Once they had received money or valuables, the bankers wrote out receipts — pieces of stone with cuneiform signs on them, corresponding to the value of the goods deposited. Thus, the valuables could be taken out by anyone upon presentation of the receipt and proving his right to ownership of that receipt (for example, with a signature or the impression of a stamp from the person who deposited the money and in whose name the receipt had been made out).

The experience of the Babylonians was then imitated in Ancient Greece»[1].

Another interesting example is the Tabularium, the most ancient and secure building in Ancient Rome. Even today, it is partially pre-

---

[1] *L.V. Orlenko.* The history of trade. Moscow, 2006. P. 108 (*Орленко Л.В.* История торговли. М., 2006. С. 108).

Stone receipt with cuneiform writing, for the depositing
of a client's valuables. Ancient Babylon, 3000 BC.

served at the base of the Capitoline hill. There lay clay tablets (tabulas)
on which certified statements for citizens' tax debts were preserved.
Because there is written evidence that in Ancient Rome one could be
put into slavery for not paying one's taxes within a set period, it is clear
that these tabulas could be sold by the State to slave owners. There is
more than one case described in which the 'mob' revolted, usually end-
ing up pillaging the Tabularium and breaking the tabulas in half.

The ancient Chinese have been credited with inventing paper money. In the 10th century China merchants stopped using the heavy iron
coins issued by the Chinese government for small purchases, and used
receipts instead. Receipts started to be used not only for depositing
coins but also for goods, for paying taxes and to issue credit. The use of
these lowered the cost of currency distribution and considerably broad-
ened trading opportunities.

The development of trade relations and wholesale trading was ham-
pered by coinage being used for major trade. When wholesale trading
developed into deals with silk convoys and ships carrying spice, sacks
and chests full of gold coins were already being used. These were not
very convenient, first of all, because of their large volume, and secondly, because of the need for reliable storage during shipping. At a time
where there were whole tribes[1] of robbers making a living from attack-
ing trade routes, things became extremely dangerous.

---

[1] Vikings, Chechens, Turks, etc.

In addition to their light weight, commercial bills of sale had one other advantage: they kept the merchant from being robbed (payment for bills of sale could only be issued to the actual person named on the endorsement).

Another important quality of the bill of sale was the cheapness and simplicity of its production — it was not necessary to buy the expensive metal kept at the mint and the assay office, it was enough just to write out the paper and endorse it.

These bills of sale were civil documents and represented the abstract obligation of the merchant or trader to pay the person indicated within a specified period the amount of the specified precious metals.

Promissory notes gave rise to a new form of currency: credit. The producer selling goods on credit received a bill of exchange (a promissory note) and could use it instead of money to pay for goods purchased from a third party.

«The rise of this type of currency as a social phenomenon only came about because capitalism established close ties between those involved in public production, much closer than those between traders»[1].

«The main types of credit currency were bills of exchange, called «trading» currency by Marx, especially transfer notes, although these could seldom be used as payment as they could not be endorsed. When this became legal (around the 17th century), they became more widely used as payment. In other words, promissory notes used as bills of exchange became recognised as methods of payment when it started being used as such. However, commercial bills of sale had several limitations on their use in domestic exchange, relating to the territory, the times, those who took part in the exchange, the nominal value (denomination) of the paper, and warranties. As a result, they could not be universally accepted. However, if we look at a range of international payments, a significant number of these were accomplished with bills of exchange: at the turn of the 20th century, these accounted for 80% of all payments. The fact that they were performing the function of world money is evident»[2].

The bill of exchange could be issued by anyone for any sum, any amount of coins or any weight of gold.

[1] *Portnoy M.A.* Aforementioned work. P. 14.
[2] *Berezina M.P.* Aforementioned work.

These two characteristics — the unlimited number of issuers and the unrestricted amount of the bill of exchange — significantly limited the acceptance of the bills, because hardly any beneficiary had reliable information about the solvency of the issuer and the amounts of the deals hardly ever matched the amounts the bills were made out to.

Gradually, the number of authorised issuers decreased and only banking establishments that dealt with promissory notes, receiving and supplying currency as part of their work were recognised, thus getting rid of the problem of unreliable issuers about whom nothing was known.

Circulation

Certified bills of exchange, as already noted, came into being for convenient circulation in major wholesale trade, and to improve and make more reliable the deposition of valuables, as well as making production cheaper and simpler. The backing for these bills was the merchant's property, either personal property, that given in exchange, or the merchant's success in trading, their caution or ability to earn money. However, improving the reliability of the depositing and keeping of valuables made circulation more difficult, as the issuers challenged endorsements which were not made out in the proper way. Every endorsement was challenged in local courts and it was possible for only the merchant who had made the endorsement to be present. Promissory regulations were therefore drawn up so that any endorser could seek damages in case an issuer refused payment. This action implied, more or less, the following: «I trusted you and accepted a bill of exchange from you for this merchant. But this merchant doesn't believe me and won't pay. Take your bill of exchange and work it out with the merchant». The circulation regulations deterred traders when there was no reliable or quick long-distance communication. Only when such communication was made possible did the promissory notes gain power as a type of money.

Merchants — known for their prudence — devised the blank endorsement, which led to the circulation of blank promissory notes for bearers and greatly simplified circulation. In this way, anyone bearing a blank promissory note became a legally bound creditor without question.

The bearers' promissory notes started a new circulation phenomenon: as derivatives, or derived securities, they allowed the bearer to make concrete transactions and this gave the bearer far more rights in relation to the issuer. Although the issue and redemption of these promissory notes complied with the law (abstract requirements for settlement), the circulation of these notes began to tie in more with the current development of property rights.

The holder of a promissory note to bearer had the right of ownership on the bill slip with an inscription, and the blank form gave an unconditional abstract right to request precious metals or coins from the debtor.

The problems with these derived secure documents and their dualist and legal nature are described in more detail in part 2.

It should be noted that the civil nature of the promissory notes only gives their holder judicial backing as opposed to State support when used as currency.

In the last decade of the 20th century, promissory notes from the Russian joint stock companies EES Russia, Gazprom and Energoatom were used to settle existing wholesale accounts, mostly because of the mistrust of the banking system which had arisen after the two system level bank crises (in 1995 and 1998).

M.P. Berezina believes in the 1990s the number of payments made without using bank funds came to 70 — 80% of all cash free payments [1].

Banknotes from private banks

Bankers' Houses replaced, not without some profit, private promissory notes with banknotes (bank bills) — bills unified by sum (face value), which was convenient and cut down on the costs of circulation (see fig. 12). In contrast with traders' promissory notes, banknotes were issued only payable to bearer and upon presentation, could be circulated over an unlimited amount of time and were backed by gold.

Such liabilities proved more reliable and became very popular, attracting the maximum demand on the market, giving their bearers an air of respectability.

[1] *M. P. Berezina.* Aforementioned work.

Percentage

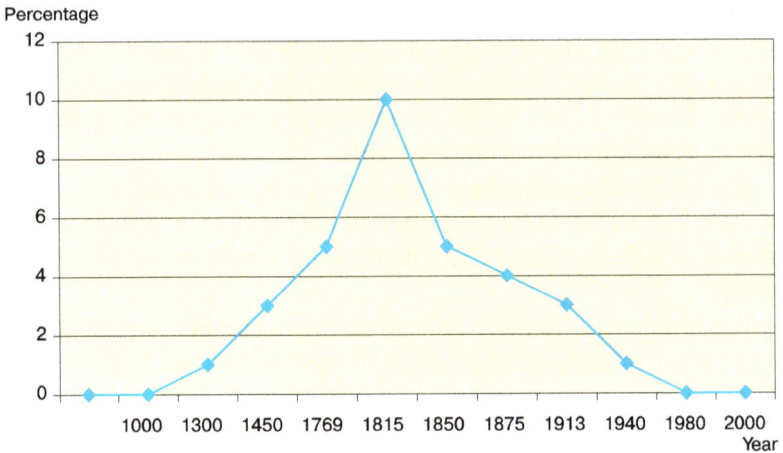

Fig. 12. Prevalence of banknotes from private banks

The Count of Monte-Cristo in Alexandre Dumas' novel of the same name boasted that he's carrying around a one-million bill from the Rothschilds, and thus greatly impressed his contemporaries.

Such *bank notes* — literally, «notes written by banks», used to be a proper noun, but became a common noun as time went by.

«A **banknote** (bank bill) — is a security unified by sum (*author's comment*), which certifies the self-addressed order of the issuing bank to pay its bearer immediately upon presentation the sum of money in coins which currently are in circulation»[1].

«A banknote is nothing else but a banker's bill, according to which the holder can receive money at any given time and which the banker uses instead of promissory notes»[2].

Even though banknotes had the same «bill nature», they were more stimulating to circulation because of the following properties:
- The broadly known wealth of the issuing banker;
- No fixed term in circulation;
- Bearer-oriented nature;

---

[1] *Russian Legal Encyclopedia.* Moscow, 1999. P. 720 (Российская юридическая энциклопедия. М., 1999. С. 720).
[2] *Marx K., Engels F.* The complete works. Vol. 25. Part 1. P. 444.

- Issue of unified sums (face values);
- Backing with gold and other bank's assets, which were considerably higher than those of traders.

Banknotes, i.e. paper money, don't have any intrinsic commodity value. Paper money is a symbol, a sign of exchange value. What then caused the permanent disappearance of gold from circulation? There must be objective causes, apart from wars and other troubles, apart from lavish rulers and cunning bankers. Here is the simplest explanation — paper money is convenient in circulation, it's easy to carry. A phrase by the great Adam Smith comes straight to the point — he said that paper money must be viewed as a cheaper circulation tool.

Consumer value of money impeded circulation, and thus to the front came exchange value, which caused a process later known as demon-etization — the withdrawing of gold, which no longer performed the functions of money, from circulation.

Circulation

Consumer value of nearly all cash credit money consisted in the quality of the paper and the engraving, which was important to those with artistic taste, but was worth only about 1 percent of its face value, which embodied the exchange value of the security in case the issuing party's business went well and the beneficiary was aware of that. If, however, the beneficiary received true or false information that the issuing party's business was experiencing difficulties, the security's exchange value would begin to decrease. Lastly, if the beneficiary believed the issuing party to be bankrupt, the security's exchange value became equal to its commodity value and depended only upon the beneficiary's artistic taste and his wish to keep this particular product of the printing industry.

A banknote from a private bank is a unified by sum «self-addressed» private bank bearer bill with a non-fixed «upon presentation» term and a blank endorsement.

This derivative security, whilst being an unconditional obligation, similar to commercial bearer bills, during its issue and paying off was subject to the law of obligations, within which it is important to specifically underline the abstract nature of an obligation, caused by the need to simplify court disputes for the benefit of trade turnover. The essence of the obligation relations which were in place during the paying off of a banknote, was the unconditional obligation to hand out a certain amount of precious metal or coins of a certain weight, composition and form.

However, circulation of such banknotes was subject to the more developed and better known at that time law of estate. The person who in the physical sense possessed the bill, undoubtedly became the creditor in this obligation case.

The bearer of a banknote had the property right to the banknote paper bill with an inscription, as well as the unconditional abstract right to demand precious metals or precious metal coins from the banker.

Banknotes were backed by the enormous — by the standards of that time — wealth of bankers. The wealth of the Rothschilds had been legendary for a long time.

It is necessary to mention that the private law nature of private banks' banknotes as a variety of bills provides their holders only with support in court, in contrast with state-endorsed private law support provided to holders of currency.

Currency

Public and legal origin

The uniqueness of currency as a form of money consists in the fact that it hasn't evolved from commodity relations and economic theories, but is designated by a State document. Its «parents» are not political economy and industrial relations, but public law — State public relations in the field of money circulation (fig. 13).

If in earlier times public relations would push forward certain commodities to be circulated as forms of money, then at present, **with public relations developed to a higher level, the public delegates the function of defining money forms to the State** (or, in some cases, the ruler himself would usurp this function) and it is the State (king, emperor, tsar, president and parliament) that define money forms on the grounds of a volitional decision.

It is the compulsion power of the State that strengthens currency. «...By Chinese laws of the 13th century, those who refused to accept

Percentage

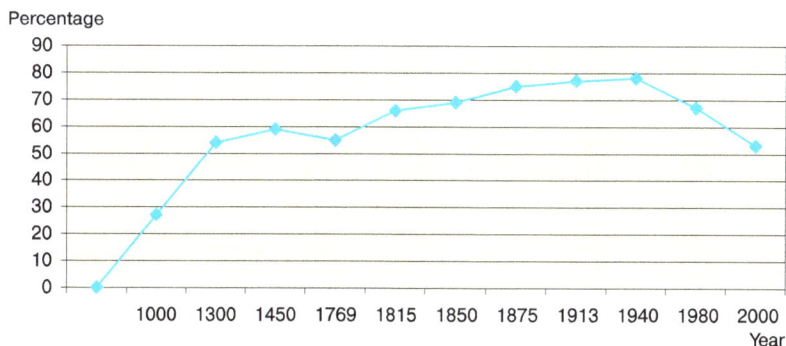

Fig. 13. Prevalence of currency

imperial paper money were sentenced to death, in France the same offence was punished by 20 years of penal servitude, and according to English legislation, refusal to accept government banknotes was seen as State treason»[1].

A revealing argument that proves the State-enforcement origin of currency is the treatment of money counterfeiting not only as a criminal, but also as a political offence. The struggle against money counterfeiting in the USA was initially led not by the police or the FBI, but the president's personal secret security service[2].

Because it is the State that issues currency, it is the State that creates additional legal norms of the public law, which are in force as well as the «usual» public law support applicable to banknotes and bills.

These additional legal norms include every trader's duty to accept currency payments, as well as more strict prosecution measures against counterfeiters compared to swindlers who forge bills and banknotes of private banks.

Aristotle, as early as in his time, made the point that «money became money (*nomisma*) not through its internal character, but on the strength of the law (*nomos*), and it is within our power to change this situation and render it useless»[3].

---

[1] *Orlenko L.V.* The history of trade. Moscow, 2006. P. 92 (*Орленко Л.В.* История торговли. М., 2006. С. 92).

[2] Similar in its tasks to the Russian Federal Guard Service.

[3] *Woelfel Ch. J.* Encyclopedia of Banking and Finance. Samara, 2000. P. 290.

The Federal Law «On currency regulation and currency control» (draft of the 29.12.1998) states the following:

1. «The currency of the Russian Federation»:

a) Roubles in the form of Central Bank of the Russian Federation bank bills (banknotes) and coins, being in circulation, as well as being or having been recalled from circulation, but still liable to exchange;

b) assets in roubles on accounts in banks and other credit institutions within the Russian Federation;

c) assets in roubles on accounts in banks and other credit institutions outside of the Russian Federation on the grounds of an agreement concluded by the Government of the Russian Federation and the Central Bank of the Russian Federation with appropriate foreign institutions about the use of Russian currency on the territory of the foreign state as a legitimate means of payment.

<...>

3. Foreign currency is:

a) monetary units such as banknotes, T-Notes, coins, being in circulation and acknowledged as the legitimate means of payment in the appropriate foreign state or group of states, as well as monetary units being or having been recalled from circulation, but still liable to exchange.

b) assets on bank accounts in monetary units of foreign states and international monetary or payment units».

As a rule, in most countries of the world national currency is defined as *provided by law for circulation liabilities of the Central Bank (Treasury, Reserve System)*, endowed by the Government with the following properties:

• it is a legal means of circulation which has to be accepted on a compulsory basis as a means of payment for goods and services on the whole territory of a country;

• it is circulated as bearer liabilities without time-limit, which exist both in cash (banknotes and coins) and non-cash form (deposit money — assets on bank accounts);

• it is acknowledged as the sole means of tax settlement;

• Government has a monopoly on its emission.

In the legal sense, one may with good reason **define modern currency as the two forms of money which act as the only acknowledged legitimate means of payment and the sole means of tax settlement:**
- **cash, or banknotes and coins of the Central Bank;**
- **non-cash, or deposit money.**

Classification of money forms on the basis of «cash — non-cash»

Let us go back to the issue of correlation of terms *money, currency, cash* and *non-cash*.

Money, i.e. property goods which function as a means of circulation, a measure of cost and a means of accumulation (preservation of cost), in Russian public practice are divided into cash and non-cash. While utilizing such terminology, we must make sure it is clearly defined.

If we **define as cash certain forms which have object content to such a measure that a man is able to hold them** (*Detencio*), we can recognize as cash the following objects:
- non-unified goods such as furs, salt, crops, metals by weight;
- unified goods such as metals, orange juice, wood, meat;
- precious metal (inc. gold) ingots of precise weight;
- ordinary bills, quasi-money in cash form, such as State bonds, fund assets, which partially function as money etc.;
- State banknotes (T-Notes) and coins;
- notes emitted by private banks.

Each of the money forms, which constitute the notion of cash money, can be contrasted with its non-cash form, that is created by the placement of the given cash form into a special repository, in order to facilitate its circulation.

It is extremely important to underline this feature. **It is the convenience of circulation, inherent to non-cash money forms, that makes a society transfer its cash forms into their non-cash equivalent**, and only a crisis of public circulation may force a society to withdraw money from appropriate repositories, but only temporarily (!). At the same time, the non-cash form doesn't disappear as an entity, simply enough its object component is minimized, becoming a paper bank statement and a data object measuring 10 000 thousand silicon domains on a magnetic bearer in an appropriate repository (bank, depository).

The term *money* includes the following notions:
* «commodity money»;
* «financial money»;
* «currency»

The first two notions have a limited circulation function, which is, however, sufficient to recognize its presence.

Each of these notion forms — respectively — has its own subforms, which can be classified on the basis of «cash — non-cash» (see Table 5).

Table 5

Classification of money forms on the basis of «cash — non-cash»

	Money form	
	Cash	Non-cash
Commodity money	non-unified goods — furs, salt, crops, metals by weight	
	unified goods — metals, orange juice, wood, meat	Non-cash contracts, taken account of by special electronic systems of commodity exchanges
	precious metal (inc. gold) ingots of precise weight	«Gold» accounts in banks and specialized depositories such as Kitco
Credit money — financial (with a limited function as a means of circulation)	Ordinary bills	Depo accounts in banks and specialized depositories.
	Quasi-money	
	Fund assets, partially functioning as money	
Credit money — currency	State banknotes (T-Notes)	Deposit money (cheque accounts)
	Central Bank coins	
	Banknotes of private banks	

It follows from Table 5 that, in particular, notes emitted by private banks, with their economic and legal content identical to currency, are mistakenly not referred by the Federal Law of 09.10.1992 № 3615-1 «On currency regulation and currency control» to the national currency of the Russian Federation.

Thus,
* the notion *currency* is a submultitude of the notion *money;*

- notions *State banknotes, Central Bank coins, notes of private banks* are submultitudes of the notion *currency*, as well as the notion *cash money*;
- the notion deposit money is a submultitude of the notion *currency*, as well as the notion *non-cash money*.

Cash currency

Percentage

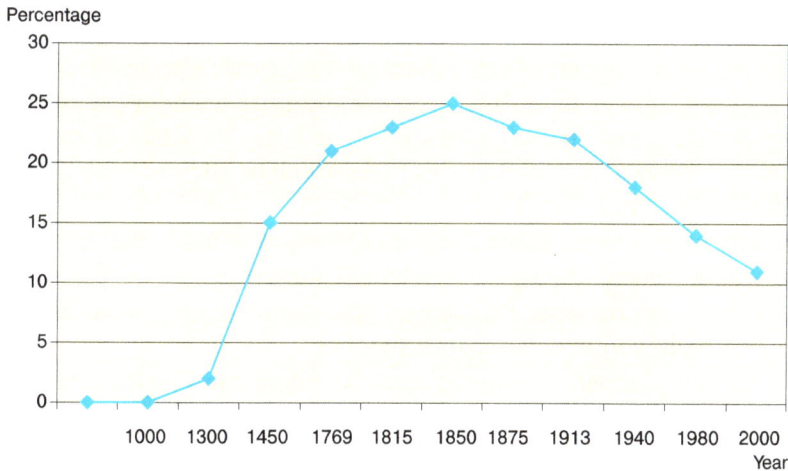

Fig. 14. Prevalence of cash currency

State banknotes (T-Notes) with full or partial metal provision

Paper money is a relative novelty in the financial world (see Fig. 15). For the first time it was put into circulation in ancient China in the IX century, when the government deprived merchants of their right to issue receipts and printed its own receipts of fixed value, which became the official replacement for coins and significantly facilitated payments. This was the first step in the world taken to form a **currency — the monetary unit of a given State, established by law**[1].

However, in other countries substitutes for «real money», i.e. coins, were broadly used as well. Their face value was confirmed by a mo-

---

[1] International currency, credit and financial relations / Ed. by L.N. Krasavina. Moscow, 2000. P. 34 (Международные валютно-кредитные и финансовые отношения / Под ред. Л.Н. Красавиной. М., 2000. С. 34).

Percent

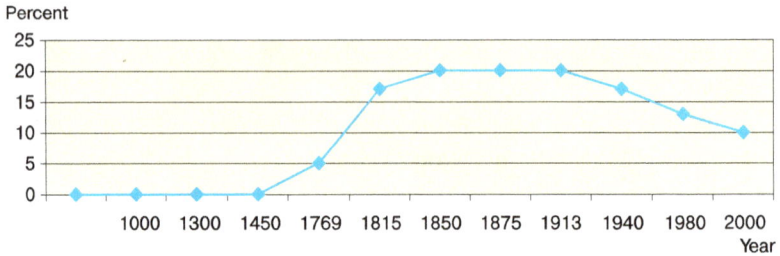

Fig. 15. Prevalence of paper money

narch's stamp or a merchant's (banker's) signature and private stamp. For example, in ancient Russia pieces of stamped leather were used for the purpose, and in 13th-century China Khubilai Khan ordered to «mint» money from mulberry tree bark, which he attested with his own Imperial stamp.

The initial causes of the evolutionary origin of banknotes lie in the following factors:

- Firstly, governments, realizing an opportunity to get gratuitous public credit, adopted merchants' practice.
- Secondly, previously minted defective billon coins logically led to a decision to replace metal as the bearer of value information with a more convenient and less expensive one, i.e. paper.

In connection with this issue, Karl Marx remarked: «In its role of a circulation intermediary, gold had experienced all sorts of misfortunes, it had been cut or even thinned until it became a simple symbolic scrap of paper»[1].

The first experiments with paper money sometimes were quite funny. «For example, the French Governor of Canada in 1658 ordered to use as money playing cards with his own signature. The reason for such decision was the fact that money from France was delivered to its colonies with a considerable delay, and settlers faced a shortage of means to pay for goods and make other settlement between each other. It was in this situation that the Governor decided to turn playing cards, which were available in abundance, into local credit money. With his signature he attested the right of the owner of such a card to exchange it for real

---

[1] *Marx K., Engels F.* The complete works. Vol. 13. P. 107–108 (*Маркс К., Энгельс Ф.* Соч. Т. 13. С. 107–108).

coins, once a ship delivering them arrives from France. The Governor's signature confirmed his duty to the owner of the card and the right of the latter to «convert» the card into real money.

Thus, plain facts themselves encouraged bankers and governments to realize that money becomes an increasingly symbolic and very cheap instrument of economic activity. Despite the fact that paper notes from bankers were merely a symbol of gold, people didn't object to using them.

Governments resorted to issuing paper money in North America in the late 17th century, i.e. earlier than in Europe. The first step was made in 1690, when the State of Massachusetts started printing paper money»[1].

In Europe, the first banknotes appeared in 1694, with the foundation of the Bank of England. By the Bank Charter Act of Robert Peel, passed in 1844, the exclusive right to issue banknotes was granted to the Bank of England only. This Act also stipulated a special system of banknote backing, which later became known as the «English» system: all currency issue, excluding a firmly fixed sum, was to be backed by the metal supply of the issuing bank, mainly by gold. The issue of banknotes not backed by metal was called *fiduciary issue*. It was the first system of partial banknote backing, which replaced the system of full backing.

In Russia, issue of banknotes was caused by a number of reasons. Coin circulation during the reign of Empress Elizabeth (1741–1761) and the following years was based on copper money, because silver and gold were in short supply at the time. The broadening of trade links, which embraced the giant territory of Russia, demanded great quantities of money of a more convenient sort than copper coins, which prevailed in circulation, but were hardly suitable for large-scale trade transactions. For instance, a payment worth 100 roubles in five-kopeck copper coins weighted as much as about 1 centner.

Issue of paper money is closely linked to certain technical and material conditions, the level of a country's productive powers, including invention and improvement of paper production, introduction of paper and other printing industry machines, availability of specialists able to provide for money production. Establishment of a special enterprise is

---

[1] *Orlenko L.V.* The history of trade. Moscow, 2006. P. 92 (*Орленко Л.В.* История торговли. М., 2006. С. 92).

also necessary. Since in Russia, until early in the 19th century, no such conditions were provided, the introduction of paper money was held back.

The first Russian document on introduction of banknotes into circulation was the «personal, given to the Senate Decree of Emperor Peter the Third of the 25th of May, year 1762»[1]. In this decree, in particular, it was stated that:

«...We haven't ceased reflecting upon invention of the most facile and reliable means, to facilitate the circulation of copper money and, in commerce itself, create a convenient and beneficial establishment of a distinguished State Bank, by which each and every person, according to their wealth and wish, for moderate interest rate, could profit, and the circulation of Bank bills to be immediately introduced, as the best means, which by many an example in Europe is verified ...»

By the same decree it was ruled that:

«1. Bank bills to be made as soon as possible for 5 000 000 roubles with various face value, viz. 10, 50, 100, 500 and 1000.

2. These bills to be printed on special paper, specifically made for the purpose, and further precautions to be taken, so that there could be no forgery.

3. For those who require the bills signed for further security, or for other necessary instructions, a new Decree is to follow immediately after this one.

4. When made, the aforementioned bills for 5 000 000 roubles to be immediately delivered to bureaucratic institutions, which distribute the greatest share of money, so that these institutions use and spend them as cash money itself, for. –

5. We wish and by this Decree command that these bills are indeed to be circulated as cash currency and as such used to pay all of Our taxes and duties, not excluding customs duties...»

Two offices of the State Bank were established in Moscow and Saint-Petersburg. However, with the instantaneous issue of bills for 5 million roubles, the bank was granted only 2 million of backing money (one in silver coins, and the other in copper coins), while the remaining 3 mil-

---

[1] The complete Laws of the Russian Empire. Vol. 15. Code: E 121/1; H, 19/3158.

lion were to be supplied from the sate treasury in the next three years (one million per year).

The Decree forbid the State Bank to «dispose of the financial capital for its own good or at its own will», but gave the following instructions: «to those who come in possession of bills, and would wish to have cash instead, cash money is to be immediately distributed upon receipt of the aforementioned bills, without any receipts and written record-keeping; and, most importantly, without any delay or red tape, or if one comes in possession of cash money, and would wish to exchange it for bills of equal value, he is to be served with the same efficiency; for this purpose, Institutions that manage this Bank are to keep a certain amount of exchanged bills... thus, the Bank will remain always inexhaustible, and the circulation of money great, fast and convenient, so that any addition to the 5 000 000 would not seem absolutely necessary, but only a result of Our extreme precaution».

The State Bank had no right to collect any commission for taking or giving out bills, so that their value in circulation was as close as possible to the value of an appropriate amount of coins.

The implementation of this Decree was declined by Catherine the Great, but the beginning of the Russo-Turkish war (1768–1774) made her issue the first paper money in the form of assignations in 1769, according to the Manifesto of the 29th of December 1768.

Specialists from Russsian Gosznak (State Administration for the Issue of Banknotes) A.E. Mikhaelis and L.A. Kharlamov argue that «they vaguely resembled money in the modern sense. **Most probably, they were bank liabilities — receipts exchangeable for coins**» (here and further bold type mine — *A.G.*)

Assignations replaced the extremely inconvenient copper money; they were highly popular and beneficial to the development of trade.

They were also used to pay civil servants' salaries. At first, all issued assignations were backed by coins and, when brought by an individual into a bank, were immediately exchanged for copper, silver or gold coins. Not long after, however, **the number of assignations began to exceed the available supply of coins, and because of the excessive assignation issue, especially during the war with Turkey, their exchange**

rate began to fall. In the last year of Catherine the Great's reign, one assignation rouble was worth only 68.5 kopecks»[1].

In France, the issue of banknotes started in 1800–1803, in Germany (then Prussia) — in 1846. Regular bankruptcies of private banks due to uncontrolled issues of banknotes, increase in social tension and aggravation of economic troubles made all European states follow the earlier example of England, i.e. impose a monopoly on banknote issue. These countries introduced a new system of banknote backing, known as the German system. In contrast with the English system, with its limit of fiduciary issue (the issue of banknotes not backed by the precious metal supply of the issuing bank), the German system envisaged a minimal quota for banknote backing. In the late 19th — early 20th century in different countries this quota made up from 50 to 30 percent of total banknote issue. Later on, yet another backing system was formed, known as the American system, the essence of which was the may so be called «doubling» of partial backing: 15 percent of banknote issue was backed by gold and, furthermore, 90 percent — by State securities. Special instructions were in place in France, where the legislator would simply determine the maximum volume of banknotes, which could be in circulation, without pointing out by what and to what percent it was backed, despite that fact that, without doubt, certain minimal backing norms did exist.

Thus, the volume of banknote issue was linked to the size of issuing banks' gold supplies, which created an opportunity to exchange banknotes for gold, which at the time acted as the monetary metal, but in periods of gold supply shortage the same factor led to financial crises. During the First World War, exchange of banknotes for gold was almost completely ceased, despite that in legislation this fact was grounded only years later. Banknotes, initially, replaced proper *money* in circulation, and then they replaced paper money as well[2].

With the introduction of paper money (in Russia — assignations), the essence of money had gone through major changes, and its double nature was confirmed once and for all. A certain object content remained — the cost of paper, ink and print. But it accounted for far less

---

[1] *Mikhaelis A.E., Kharlamov L.A.* Russian paper money. Perm, 1993. P. 3 (*Михаэлис А.Э., Харламов Л.А.* Бумажные деньги России. Пермь, 1993. С. 3).
[2] See: Russian Legal Encyclopedia. Moscow, 1999 (Российская юридическая энциклопедия. М., 1999).

than the actual value of a banknote (assignation). The Central Bank's promise to pay gold for the assignation became its main value component. Usually, this would be a gold bill of the Central Bank[1]. On pre-Revolution Russian banknotes one may read: «This bill is exchanged upon presentation for ... parts of pure gold».

Circulation

The previously described banknote issued by a private bank by both its economic nature and its derivative object content, and also by its primary liability content greatly differs from a State banknote.

In case with issue and repayment of State banknotes, not private law, but public law was in force. The essence of liability relations, which arose when a banknote was paid off, was either an unconditional obligation to give out a certain quantity of precious metal or coins of certain weight, content and form, or an unconditional obligation of the government to accept the banknote as the means of paying taxes and customs fees.

The derivative proprietary right of circulation also changed, it was confirmed by the public law obligation to accept money in certain form during all trade operations as the means of payment, which is to be accepted on a compulsory basis. This right of the bearer was supported by the power (the capacity for legal compulsion) of the State.

Cash currency is guaranteed by the property of the State and its Central Bank, by the State's right to collect taxes.

The holder of a State banknote not only had a proprietary right in the paper note, but also the right to use this note to make *any* payment anywhere within the country. The banknote symbolizes an unconditional abstract right to demand precious metals or precious metal coins from the State or an abstract right to use the banknote for tax payment.

The holder's right to accept payment is replaced by the issuing party's duty to accept payment.

State banknotes (T-notes) not backed by metal

In 1762, in order to put the first paper money into circulation as soon as possible, a new requirement in Moscow and Saint-Petersburg

---

[1] «At present not a single country retains the possibility to exchange banknotes for gold» (R. Barr. Aforementioned work. P. 288).

prescribed at least 20 percent of tax payments' sum total to be made in 25-rouble assignations[1].

At the time, credit money in Russia had already developed into **currency — the monetary unit of a certain country stipulated by law, the sole means of tax settlement and repayment of State credits.**

«Credit, too, as a public form of wealth, forces money out[2] and usurps its place»[3].

V.A. Byelov describes currency as follows: «...objects, which conform to legal requirements and are accepted by the State as the sole means of payment with a compulsory exchange-value, and take the form of a national monetary unit.

Paper money is yet another kind of monetary unit, identical to billon coins by its economic nature. Face value of paper money was considerably higher than their cost as objects (paper notes made and dyed by a certain method). Money circulation was provided for by the State, which established and protected its compulsory exchange-value, i.e. its obligatory acceptance for all payments at its nominal cost.

Banknotes (bank notes and bills; in Russia, one also points out assignations [1769–1849] and credit bills [1841–1919]) are bank bills (in Russia — only State banks or the Treasury) in the form of self-addressed orders to pay their bearer immediately upon presentation the amount of money, indicated as a round number, in small coins of full value or paper money. By their economic nature, these are transferable self-addressed bearer bills, with the payment date specified as «upon presentation»... In England, the first attempt was made to regulate the issue of such documents. Bankers' self-addressed bills became known as «bank notes» and a special system of legal regulations was also created. The usage of promissory notes in inner market circulation began to dwindle. Moving into international trade and replacing money and monetary units, in inner circulation promissory notes themselves were replaced by receipts»[4].

---

[1] *Katz L.Z., Malyshev V.P.* Russian Paper Monetary Units Encyclopedia, Vol. 1. Saint-Petersburg, 1998. P. 591 (*Кац Л.З., Малышев В.П.* Энциклопедия бумажных денежных знаков России. Т. 1. СПб., 1998. С. 591).
[2] Apparently, Marx talks about natural commodity money — gold, silver etc.
[3] *Marx K., Engels F.* The complete works. Vol. 25. Part 11. P. 121.
[4] *Byelov V.A.* On currency convertibility // *Business and banks*, 1996. Issue 26 (*Белов В.А.* Кое-что о конвертируемости валют // *Бизнес и банки*, 1996. № 26).

Money, which is deprived of its intrinsic value, is called «decreted», or paper money. The Anglo-American term is *fiat money,* and it derives from *fiat* — decree, edict; because paper money is put into circulation by a Government decree. For instance, we may compare the official paper dollars (printed to order of the USA Government) and paper dollars used in the «Monopoly» board game (printed by *Parker Brothers game company*). Why only the official paper dollars are suitable for buying things in the real world? The answer is obvious: because the USA Government announced that these dollars are a legitimate means of payment and on each of them it is said that: «This note is legal tender for all debts, public and private»[1].

An episode from the reign of Holy Roman Emperor Frederick II (1194–1250), described by L.V. Orlenko, is a curious example. The Emperor tried to make his subjects accept gilded leather «augustals» at the nominal value of gold[2]. However, without a firmly defined legal base and the State's real authority, the attempt was doomed.

«Reflecting on the general abandonment of the gold standard in money circulation, we must note that the role of gold in the period of capitalism is quite ambivalent. On the one hand, it's always in view and is perceived by the society as the sole form of full value money, and also as the embodiment of wealth. On the other hand, it isn't anymore the only available form of money and is forced to share this role with the offspring of capitalism — the rapidly progressing credit money. The ambivalent role of gold has been hidden for a long period of time, because credit money emerges and develops on the base of gold, performs an increasing amount of work, but without the dramatic effects that accompany the functioning of gold at the time.

In a capitalist society the role of money in the economic process undergoes drastic changes. In the epoch of trade money played an intermediate part in a trade agreement as a means of circulation and payment, as well as a means of wealth accumulation. However, at present the main role of money is to be the necessary prerequisite for and the starting point of capital turnover, and then an essential part of capital.

---

[1] *Mankiw N.G.* Aforementioned work. P. 589.
[2] See: *Orlenko L.V.* The history of trade. Moscow, 2006. P. 91 (*Орленко Л.В.* История торговли. М., 2006. С. 91).

Money is necessary to put productive capital to work, to get it moving and constantly keep it moving. To achieve this, money must be constantly moving itself. However, this is not a basic movement, but a movement during which the value of capital grows, thus, the sum of money that represents this value must grow to an equal measure.

Gold turns out to be unfit for this task. One is forced to provide for accumulation of the sum of money, which represents the growing value of capital, in a mechanical way, i.e. by increasing the mass of collected gold. With the development of capitalism, especially with the approach of the industrial capitalism era, it is immediately discovered that there's simply not enough gold! More and more gold must be mined just for the purpose of minting coins and putting them into circulation. All this effort, apparently, is almost entirely useless, because money only serves the movement of capital, acting — as «the uninitiated» see it — as the unavoidable, but unavailing intermediary, with whose presence on the stage of economic life one has to put up.

A significant amount of gold can be saved when paper money, convertible into gold, is used in circulation. However, even in this case there's not enough gold. The motif of the insufficiency of gold for monetary purposes is constantly present in economic works on this subject throughout the 19th — early 20th centuries.

That despite the shortage of gold, the monetary system was still able to fulfill its tasks, is explained by the fact that since its very onset capitalism creates and puts into its own service more and more credit money, which, instead of gold, successfully serves a growing number of settlements. However, because this credit money exists on paper, because it has to use paper as its bearer, contemporaries don't recognize it as independent money of a new, higher degree, but perceive it as simple paper money convertible into gold, which serves only as the replacement of gold in circulation. This confusion is in place up to present date, when the term «credit-paper money» is used in economic literature when referring to modern credit money»[1].

«The reasons why real money (silver and gold coins) were forced out of circulation by unchangeable paper money are often explained by the fact that gold serves barter only transiently, turning into ideal money. Money circulation itself separates the real content of a coin from its

---

[1] See: *Portnoy M.A.* Aforementioned work.

nominal content, separates its metal being from its functional being. In circulation itself already there is a hidden opportunity to replace metal money by its function, replace coins by monetary units made from other materials or just by basic symbols. Thus, paper money originates from the function of money as the means of circulation»[1]. Credit money originates at a certain stage of commodity production development, when payment by installments becomes widespread. In K. Marx's *Capital* credit money[2] is defined as money in the form of a liability[3].

Circulation

Banknotes and coins of the Central Bank are defined as unified by sum «self-addressed» State bearer bills with their term defined as «upon presentation» and with a blank endorsement.

In contrast with the previous type of banknotes, the right to claim gold in exchange for the banknote has been lost. All the other properties have remained.

As well as the bearer of a banknote with metal backing, the bearer of a State banknote without metal backing not only has the proprietary right to the paper note with the inscription itself, but also possesses the right to make by this note *any* payment within the country. However, contrary to the first case, the State banknote embodies only the unconditional abstract right to be presented as a means of payment in the situation of paying tax.

Coins with nominal value

Money with nominal value must be considered separately as an example of natural money evolving into credit money (fig. 16).

It is believed that the first of the best-known attempts to introduce credit money was made by Emperor Nero, who decreased the content of gold in coins (common folk at the time believed he was «spoiling» coins). Thus, for the first time in history the value of metal in a coin became lower than its nominal value, but still was high enough to define consumer properties of metal.

---

[1] See: *Marx K.* Capital. A Critique of Political Economy. Vol. 1 // Marx K., Engels F. The complete works. Vol. 23. Moscow, 1960. P. 136.
[2] Ibidem. P. 151.
[3] *Efimova L.G.* Is tax payment by «dead» money a possibility? // *Business and banks*, 1998. October issue (*Ефимова Л.Г.* Возможна ли уплата налогов «мертвыми» деньгами? // *Бизнес и банки*, 1998. Окт).

Percentage

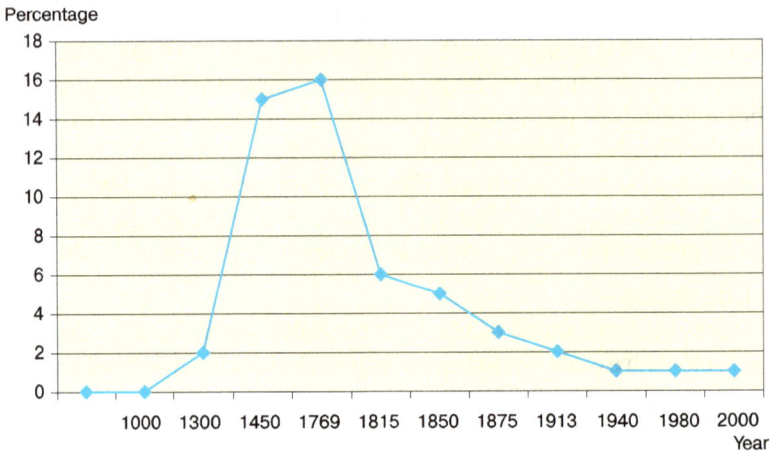

Fig. 16. Prevalence of coins with nominal value

Gold, circulating as jewelry, at present is always mixed with copper, silver, nickel and zinc to increase its shine and durability. Consumer properties of such gold improve, but its exchange value as the gold-containing metal decreases. Thus, if gold was «diluted» by other metals to an insignificant measure, there was no social controversy. However, as soon as this proportion exceeded the limits of what was accepted by the public conscience, unrest grew and riots sprung up — thus the society tried to make the State executives change their viewpoint.

«At first coin minting was a private trade (in Russia, for example, coin minters were known as "livtsy" — "casters" and "serebryaniki" — "silversmiths"). Then minting was monopolized by the State and coin production began at State premises known as Mints.

In the world of ancient civilizations, as has already been stated above, coins were made from pure silver and gold (Greece) or their alloy (Lydia). Then they started adding hardeners (for instance, copper in gold alloys). Too high an amount of hardener resulted in coin spoiling.

Coin spoiling by the State is a deliberate act of decreasing the weight or the standard of coins while preserving their face value, in order to get profit[1]. This means that, together with the monopoly on coin minting, the State got the opportunity to spoil coins.

---

[1] In the form of the difference between the liability content and the object content of money.

Money as an economic and value category 109

The decrease of the amount of metal in coins is usually more or less palpable and is achieved by various means. For example, it is done by simply decreasing the weight of freshly minted coins without any damage to the quality of metal or by spoiling the metal, mixing it with a cheap additive, whilst the weight of coins either stays the same or increases. Also, sometimes a precious metal is simply replaced by a non-precious one.

Coin spoiling was broadly practiced in slave-trading and feudal societies, especially during wars which put all involved parties in a tense financial situation. Thus, in Rome the weight of coins was a kind of barometer, which indicated periods, when tyrannical power of the Emperor, or social unrest, significantly increased. Historians provide us with the following evidence: a silver denarius during the reign of Augustus (63 BC — AD 14) weighed 3.89g; in Nero's time (37—68), its weight went down to 3.41g and 15 percent of additive was mixed in. In Commodus' time (161—192), it weighed 2.85g and the amount of additive had grown up to 50 percent; at Septimius Severus' time (146—211), it's already up to 60 percent, and an old denarius is now twice as expensive as a new one. Quite often coins had a copper core, covered with thin silver plating. This was nothing else but official counterfeiting of coins»[1].

It was coin spoiling that demonstrated the State's power. Common folk and traders accepted these coins because, on the one hand, it was acceptable for paying taxes, and, on the other, apparently, the State could force traders to accept this and no other money as the means of payment for their goods.

Coins began to differentiate into full-value coins and change. Full-value coins are a type of monetary unit in the form of an ingot (usually round-shaped), made from an alloy containing a precious metal. Face value of a full-value coin was equal to the value of the amount of precious metal contained in it. Billon coins are another sort of monetary units, looking the same as full-value coins, but, in contrast to the latter, their face value was higher than the value of the alloy they were made from, as well as higher than their production cost.

[1] *Orlenko L.V.* The history of trade. Moscow, 2006. P. 90 (*Орленко Л.В.* История торговли. М., 2006. С. 90).

Copper coins (fig.17) nominated in silver, minted in the time of Russian Tsar Nicholas I (1840), can serve as an example[1].

Fig. 17. Coins, issued in Russia in 1840 (copper): $^1/_4$ kopeck in silver (1.7g), $^1/_2$ kopeck in silver (5.1g), 1 kopeck in silver (10.2g), 2 kopecks in silver (20.4g), 3 kopecks in silver (30.7g)

In Russia, coin spoiling by Princes and Tsars, spoiling of silver «grivnas» by cutting off pieces and the emergence of «thief» money led to complete disappearance of full-weight coins, social unrest and riots («copper riot» in the time of Tsar Alexei Mikhailovich in the mid.-17th century) Trying to avoid difficulties, the government began to mint copper money with an enforced exchange rate. As a result, the market value of the silver rouble began to grow compared to its face value, silver almost entirely disappeared from circulation and was hoarded by money-lenders and money-changers, and commodity prices in general went up.

Difficulties experienced by «bimetallic» countries are explained by Copernicus-Gresham's Law, discovered in 1526 by the Polish scholar Nicolaus Copernicus and in 1560 by the English financier Sir Thomas Gresham: «Bad money drives good money out of circulation»[2]. This means, that if two kinds of coins, interconnected by a legal correlation of exchange, are in circulation in the same country at the same time, there arises the trend for disappearance of the better (in terms of their

---

[1] *Krivtsov V.D.* Aforementioned work. P. 71.
[2] *Anikin A.V.* Economics and Finance English-Russian Dictionary. Saint-Petersburg, 1993 (*Аникин А.В.* Англо-русский словарь по экономике и финансам. СПб., 1993).

commercial value) coins. What happens is precisely this: good money is either hoarded or used in foreign trade, or remelted and then exchanged for bad money.

Eventually, copper money was withdrawn from circulation. In the late 17th century, the amount of silver in rouble coins was decreased by 30%. In Russia, up until the 17th century, mining of precious metals was extremely underdeveloped, and because of that Mints, which in the 17th century were monopolized by the State, remelted foreign coins. According to the «monetary regalia» of Peter the Great, export of precious metal bars was strictly banned, whilst export of spoilt coins was allowed.

As the price of the precious metal component in coins with low face value continues to grow, there arises a problem of the object component of coin value being higher than its liability component.

«The Swiss Government decided, from the 1st of January 2007, to withdraw from circulation one-centime coins (0.0076 US dollars). It costs 11 centimes to produce a one-centime coin, as Hans-Rudolf Merz, Head of the Federal Department of Finance, has calculated. His plan included saving another 230 500 dollars by eliminating five-centime coins as well, but consumer organizations, fearing that round numbers on price tags would in fact mean growth of prices, won the fight to save five-centime coins.

The cost of metal content in United States one-cent coins (97.5% zinc core, 2.5% copper plating) rose up to 77% of their face value. Also, if one adds the minting and distribution costs (0.0061 dollars per one cent), it turns out that the United States Mint's costs involved in producing a one-cent coin exceed its face value by 38%. The US cent has been through this before: in 1982 the cost of its copper content exceeded its face value, and as a result the coin's weight was lessened from 3.1 to 2.5 grams, and the copper content was reduced from 95 to 2.5%.

The five-cent coin weighting 5g (75% copper, 25% nickel) costs Americans 4.5 cents, or 5.75 cents including production costs, which exceeds the face value by 15%.

The value of metal content in Russian coins may also be higher than their face value... But the information on metal content in Russian coins is restricted... In Russia, too, the cost of metal content is close to the face value. In a one-kopeck coin metal content exceeds its face value by over 100% percent... In the early 1990-ies the Central Bank of Russia even had to cease minting small change, as the then First Deputy to the Central Bank President Arnold Voilukov confessed in 2003: «Our coins contain copper and nickel, and thus reminting them even with the help of rather primitive technologies would be profitable».

Even paper money may turn out to be cheaper than the material it is made of. The catastrophic inflation that hit Germany in 1922 (prices were multiplied by 5570) and 1923 (by 1300 billion) made banknotes more expensive than paper. And in 2003, a Web portal for travelers Inyourpocket.com, calculated that in Byelorussian restrooms it is cheaper to use one-rouble bills than toilet paper. However, in 2004 President Lukashenko withdrew one-rouble banknotes from circulation»[1].

Liability nature of cash currency

It is easy to see that at the present stage of economic development the term «currency» refers not to an object as such, which has certain consumer value, but to an abstract formal obligation of a country's Central Bank, which only has certain exchange value, created by the demand for currency to pay taxes[2].

Money in the form of currency is a particular variety of a bill, which, in its turn, is a security (Article 143 of the Civil Code of the Russian Federation). Further on, when we use the term «currency», let us consider the fact that it is a security (fig. 18).

Sir John Richard Hicks in his classic work «Value and Capital» observed that: «A security of any sort, which brings in a fixed interest... is a promise to pay a certain sum of money in the future. However, there are certain types of documents, which contain an obligation, the documents that aren't usually referred to as securities, but considered to be money itself, though the same classification applies to them. Bank deposits, at present usually referred to as money, are a promise to pay money in the future; even banknotes are a promise to pay money. Such

---

[1] *Grozovsky B., Soukhmansky M.* More expensive than money // *Vedomosti*, 2006. Issue 69 (1596). 19th of April (*Грозовский Б., Сухманский М.* Дороже денег // *Ведомости*, 2006. № 69 (1596). 19 апр.).

[2] From the above it is clearly concluded that the stability of currency depends mainly on the state's tax-collecting capacity.

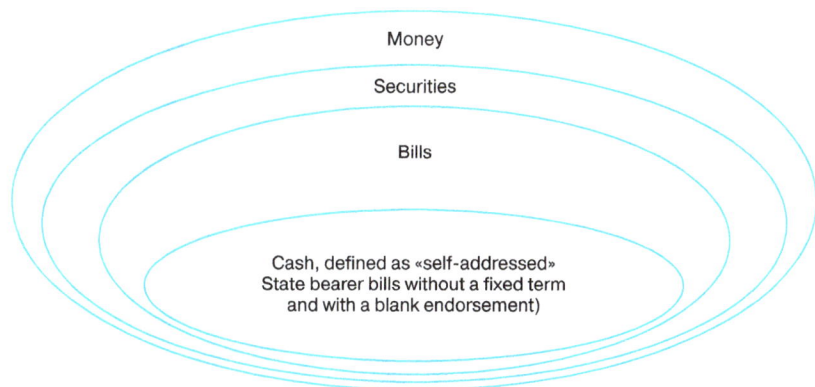

Fig. 18. Money — securities — bills — cash

nature of banknotes doesn't require any explanations and is perceptible to common sense in cases when banknotes represent a promise to pay certain... money (gold or bank bills of some other bank superior in influence to the given bank). However, if superior money disappears from circulation, a paradoxical situation arises. And this paradoxicality reflects the very essence of the problem, it is definitely not incidental. It is a blessing — to have a constant reminder about this paradox in the form of the inscription on the one-pound banknote: "The Bank of England promises to pay the bearer on demand the sum of one pound sterling"»[1].

On pound sterling banknotes it is legibly written: «*Bank of England. I promise to pay the bearer on demand the sum of...*». This is followed by a signature of the of the Chief Cashier of the Bank of England. By its form and content this is a **State bearer promissory note with an «upon presentation» term.**

On USA banknotes, there is no direct promise, but signatures of the Treasurer and the US Secretary of the Treasury are present. However, on old American banknotes, for example on Greenbacks of 1862, there is an inscription: «*will pay the bearer on demand*».

---

[1] *Hicks J.R.* Value and Capital. Moscow: Progress, 1993. P. 277.

On 10-dollar Canadian banknotes dating back to 1906 it is also in-scribed: «*will pay the bearer on demand*».

On Scottish banknotes of 177 is was written that: «*Royal Bank of Scotland hereby obliged to pay the bearer on demand ... by order of the court of Directors*».

Old Russian banknotes leave no doubt as to their nature: on ban-knotes between 1779 and 1830 was written: «St. Petersburg Bank pays the bearer of this government **assignat** (author's bold — A.G.) ...in rouble currency, in the year of...» The year of the currency was even shown, insofar as the content of precious metals in it changed depend-ing on the year of minting[1]. On the 1779 banknote the four signatures

---

[1] The year of minting was no longer printed on banknotes after the war of 1812.

St. Petersburg Bank zhalrich the bearer of this government assignat
100 units of rouble currency. 1779. St Petersburg.

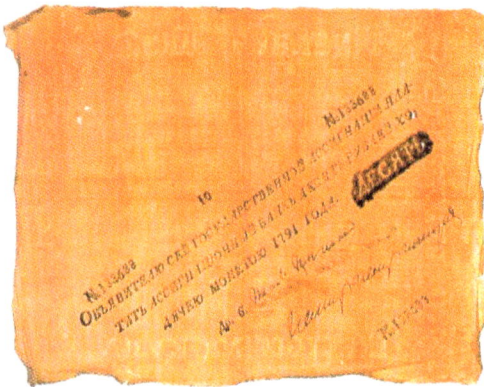

The assignor bank pays the
bearer of this government
assignat 10 units of rouble
currency. 1791.

37.

№4678693

25

ОБЪЯВИТЕЛЮ СЕЙ ГОСУДАРСТВЕ-
ННОЙ АССИГНАЦІИ ПЛАТИТЪ АССИ-
ГНАЦІОННЫЙ БАНКЪ ДВАДЦАТЬ
ПЯТЬ РУБЛЕЙ ХОДЯЧЕЮ МОНЕТОЮ
1811 ГОДА. ДВАДЦАТЬ ПЯТЬ

Др. б.

№4678693   №4678693

The assignor bank pays the bearer of this government assignat 25 units of rouble currency. 1811.

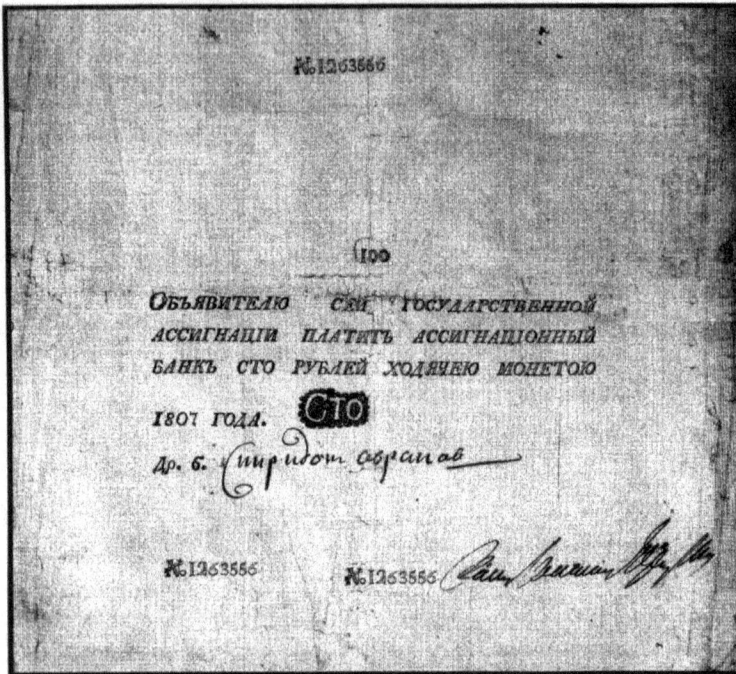

The assignor bank pays the bearer of this government assignat 100
units of rouble currency. 1807.

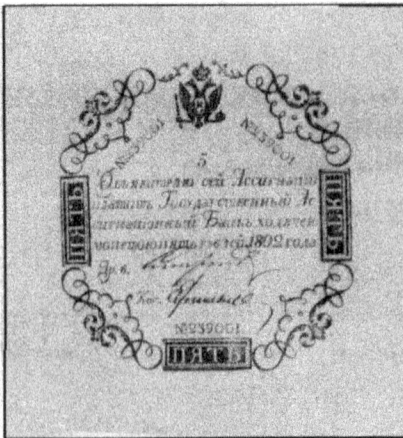

The state assignor bank pays
the bearer of this government
assignat five units of rouble
currency. 1802.

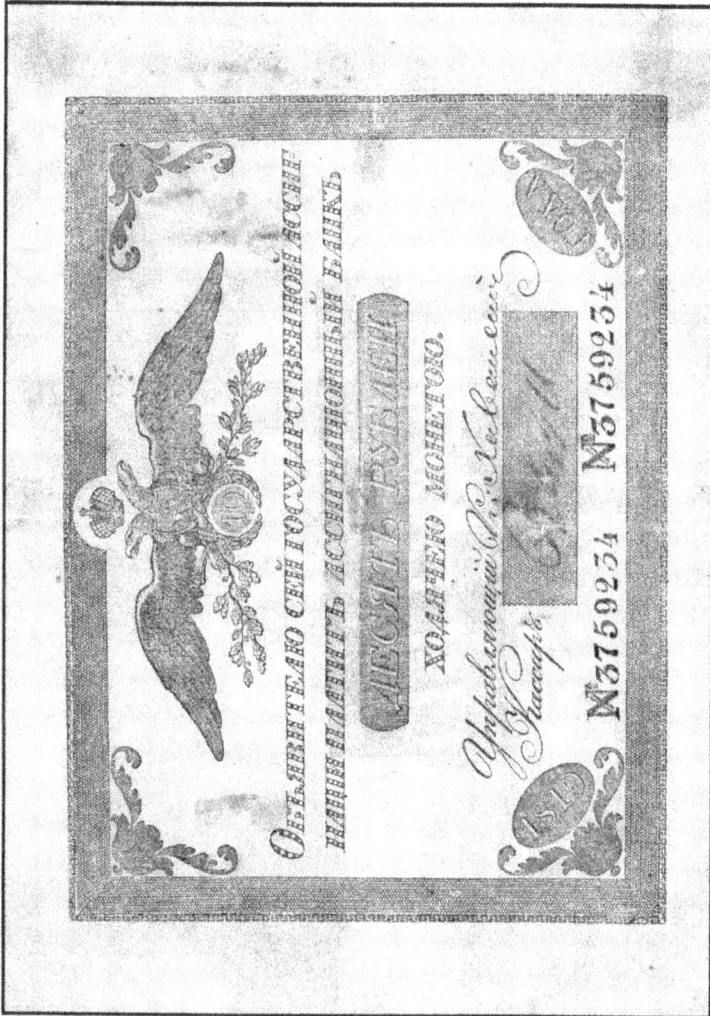

The assignor bank pays the bearer of this government assignat 10 units of rouble currency. Opravlyaushi...

The assignor bank pays the bearer of this government assignat 25 units of rouble currency. Opravlyaushi...

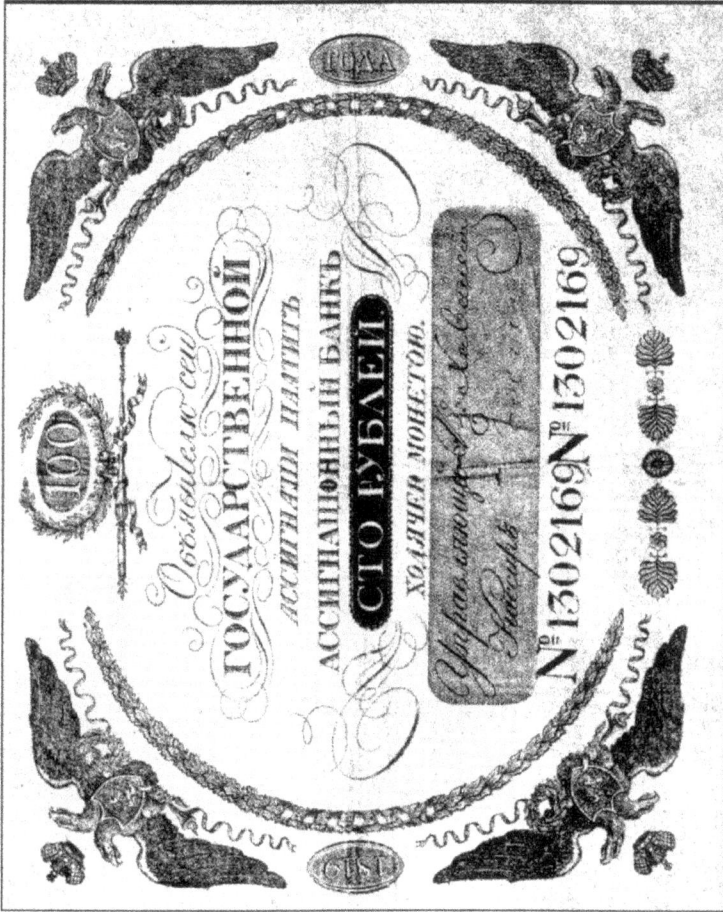

The assignor bank pays the bearer of this government assignat 100 units of rouble currency.

ГОСУДАРСТВЕННЫЙ

Коммерческій Банкъ

1840.

№320505

1840.

№320505

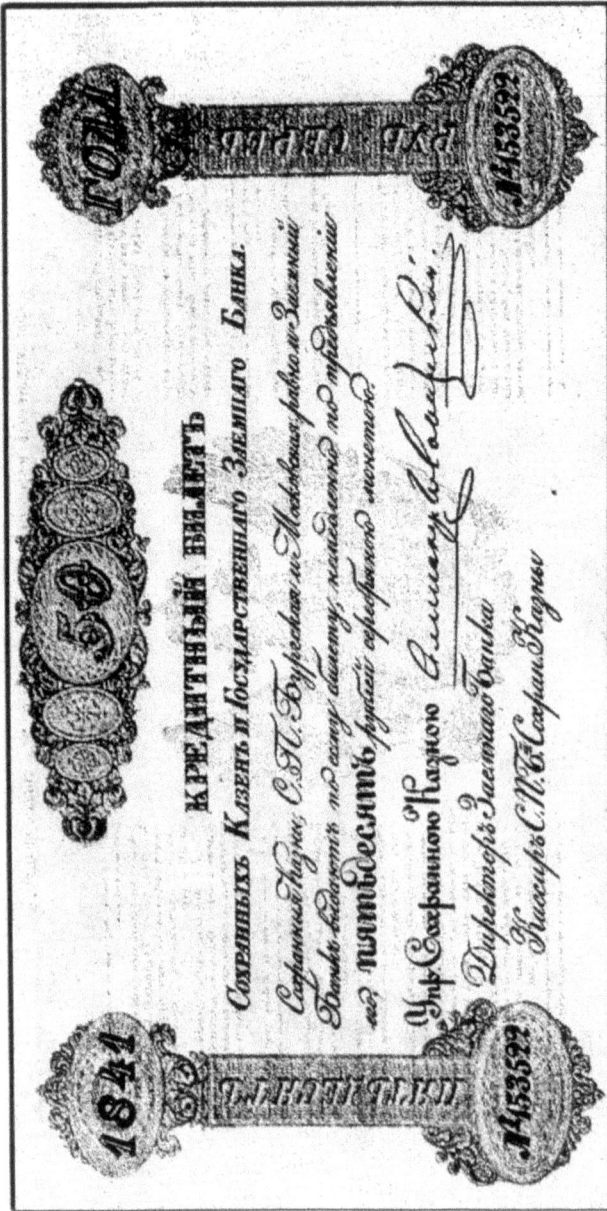

Credit note . of the Savings Treasuries and the State Lending Bank . The Savings Treasuries, S. P. Burgskaya and Moscow and the Lending Bank alike will issue, in accordance with this note, immediately on presentation (of the note), 50 roubles in silver currency.

Administered by the Saving Treasury: signature
Director of the Lending Bank
Cashier S.P.B. of the Savings Treasury

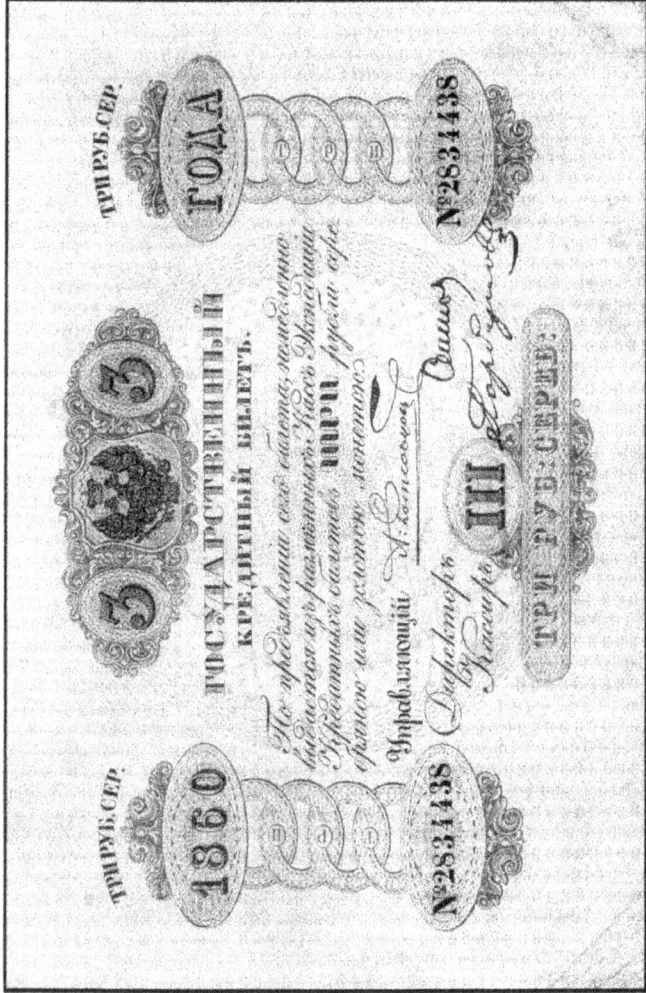

State. Credit Note. On presentation of this note, THREE roubles in silver or gold currency will immediately be issued from the exchange funds

Administrator	signature
Director	signature
Cashier	signature

State Credit Note. 1855. One rouble in Silver.
The Cashier of Credit Notes Expedition immediatly pays the bearer
One rouble in Silver or in Gold coin

Administrator   signature
Cashier   signature

State Credit Note. 1860. Five roubles in Silver.
The Cashier of Credit Notes Expedition immediatly pays the bearer
Five roubles in Silver or in Gold coin

Administrator   signature

Cashier   signature

State Credit Note. Three roubles in Silver or Gold Coins.
The Exchange Cashier of the State Bank pays the bearer Three roubles
in Silver or Gold Coins

Administrator   signature

Cashier   signature

State Credit Note. Five roubles in Silver or Gold Coins.
The Exchange Cashier of the State Bank pays the bearer Five roubles
in Silver or Gold Coins

Administrator   signature

Cashier   signature

The State Bank exchanges credit notes for gold currency without limit on the sum (1 rouble= 1/15 of an imperial unit and contains 17,424 dolias of pure gold).

ГОСУДАРСТВЕННЫЙ БАНКЪ РАЗМѢНИВАЕТЪ
КРЕДИТНЫЕ БИЛЕТЫ НА ЗОЛОТУЮ МОНЕТУ
БЕЗЪ ОГРАНИЧЕНІЯ СУММЫ
(1 РУБЛЬ = 1/15 ИМПЕРІАЛА, СОДЕРЖИТЪ
17,424 ДОЛЕЙ ЧИСТАГО ЗОЛОТА)

The exchange of government credit notes for gold currency is secured by all
property of the State.

1. РАЗМѢНЪ ГОСУ-
ДАРСТВЕННЫХЪ КРЕ-
ДИТНЫХЪ БИЛЕТОВЪ
НА ЗОЛОТУЮ МОНЕТУ
ОБЕЗПЕЧИВАЕТСЯ ВСѢМЪ
ДОСТОЯНІЕМЪ ГОСУДАРСТВА
2. ГОСУДАРСТВЕННЫЕ КРЕДИТНЫЕ БИЛЕТЫ
ИМѢЮТЪ ХОЖДЕНІЕ ВО ВСЕЙ ИМПЕРІИ
НАРАВНѢ СЪ ЗОЛОТОЮ МОНЕТОЮ.

Government credit notes are to be accepted throughout the Empire, on an
equal par with gold currency. "

1. The exchange of state credit notes for gold currency is guaranteed by all state property
2. State credit notes are valid throughout the Empire, on a par with gold currency
3. As a result of counterfeiting credit notes the guilty parties lose all rights to property and will face exile to a hard labour camp.

One Rouble

The State Bank exchanges Credit Notes for gold currency without limit on the sum
(1 rouble= 1/15 of an imperial unit and contains 17.424 dolias of pure gold)

Manager [signed]
Cashier [signed]

1. The exchange of state credit notes for gold currency is guaranteed by all state property
2. State credit notes are valid throughout the Empire, on a par with gold currency
3. As a result of counterfeiting credit notes the guilty parties lose all rights to property and will face exile to a hard labour camp.

Three Roubles

The State Bank exchanges Credit Notes for gold currency without limit on the sum
(1 rouble= 1/15 of an imperial unit and contains 17.424 dolias of pure gold)

Manager [signed]
Cashier [signed]

1. The exchange of state credit notes for gold currency is guaranteed by all state property
2. State credit notes are valid throughout the Empire, on a par with gold currency
3. As a result of counterfeiting credit notes the guilty parties lose all rights to property and will face exile to a hard labour camp.

State Credit Note

Five Roubles

The State treasury exchanges credit notes for pounds sterling, without limit
on the sum, according to the exchange rate 40 roubles=1 pound sterling

1. The exchange of state credit notes for gold currency is guaranteed by all state property
2. State credit notes are valid throughout the Empire, on a par with gold currency
3. As a result of counterfeiting credit notes the guilty parties lose all rights to property and will face exile to a hard labour camp.

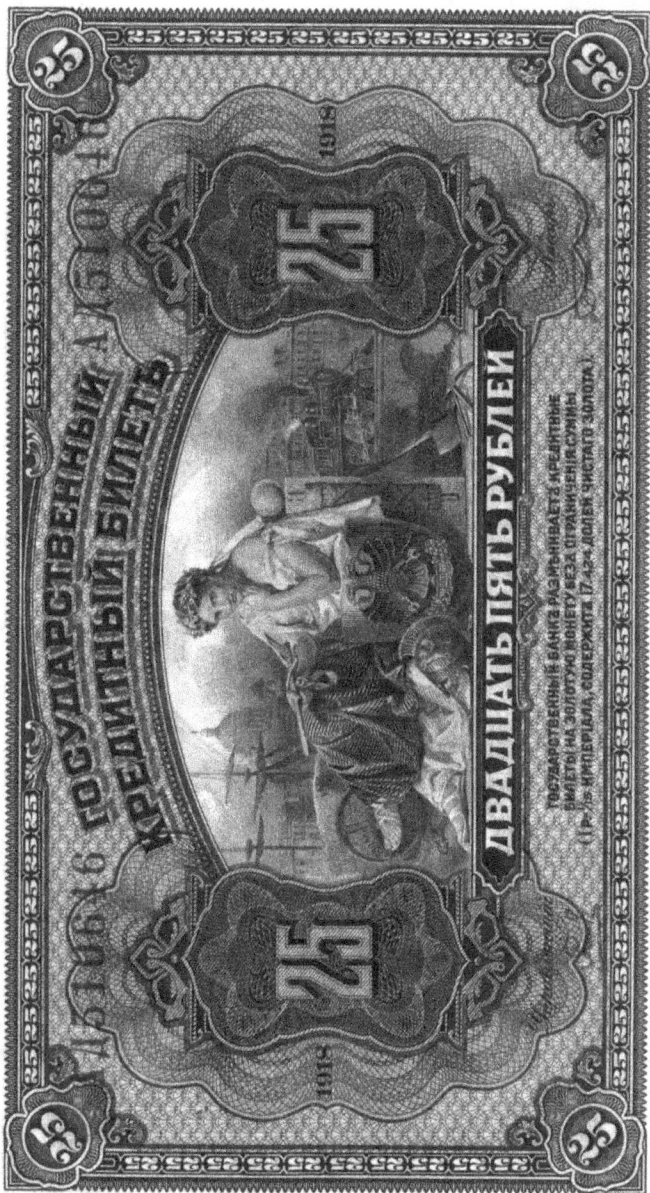

Twenty-Five Roubles

The State Bank exchanges credit notes for gold currency without limit on the sum (1 rouble= 1/15 of an imperial unit and contains 17,424 dolias of pure gold).

1. The exchange of state credit notes for gold currency is guaranteed by all state property
2. State credit notes are valid throughout the Empire, on a par with gold currency
3. As a result of counterfeiting credit notes the guilty parties lose all rights to property and will face exile to a hard labour camp.

Twenty-Five Roubles

The State Bank exchanges credit notes for gold currency without limit on the sum (1 rouble= 1/15 of an imperial unit and contains 17,424 dolias of pure gold)

Manager [signed]

Cashier [signed]

1. The exchange of state credit notes for gold currency is guaranteed by all state property

2. State credit notes are valid throughout the Empire, on a par with gold currency

3. As a result of counterfeiting credit notes the guilty parties lose all rights to property and will face exile to a hard labour camp.

(of the two senators, the chief director of the board of banks and the director of the local bank) only appeared handwritten and only in ink[1].

From 1840, the word «pays» was replaced by the word «issues».

On the reverse of banknotes of the period between 1855 and 1872, the following excerpts were printed from the High Manifesto: «**Government credit notes are provided for** (author's bold — *A.G.*) by all of the State's property and by exchange, unceasing at any time, for coin currency from the predetermined fund»[2].

On «tenners» in 1909, the front of the banknote bore the inscription: «The State Bank exchanges **credit notes** (author's bold — *A.G.*) for gold coins without a limit on the sum (1 rouble = $^1/_{15}$ of an imperial, contains 17.424 parts of pure gold)». On the reverse of the banknote was inscribed: «The exchange of government credit notes for gold currency is secured by all of the State's property. Government credit bills are valid throughout the Empire, on a par with gold coins.»

It was even written on Soviet banknotes, up to 1991, that they were secured by the gold reserves of the country or «all of the Republic's property», and the Bolsheviks themselves in 1921 issued currency in 1.5

---

[1] *V.D. Krivtsov.* Averse: Catalogue for Collectors. M., 1999. P. 81 (*Кривцов В.Д.* Аверс: Каталог для коллекционеров. M., 1999. C. 81).
[2] Ibidem.

and 10 billion rouble notes called «Obligations of the R.S.F.S.R.»[1] In 1924 «Payment Liabilities»[2] were issued.

The direct indication either to a liability, or to a security demonstrates to us the liability character of paper money.

The judicial system's mixture of property and other (mainly obligatory) rights in Russia today can in many ways be explained by the influence of Anglo-American legal concepts. In this system of law it is accepted to differentiate «things in possession» (*choses in possession*) i.e. things which can be physically possessed, and «things in demand» (*choses in action*), i.e. various rights (which in turn can be regarded as a literal interpretation of the phrase «intangible assets» — *res incorporales,* from Roman civil law). However in the European, continental legal system, the regime of property and the regime of rights are clearly differentiated. Thus, Art. 90 of the German Civil Code directly decrees that only «tangible objects» can be things.

Whilst investigating the current, tangible make-up of paper money, it is possible to introduce an interesting example. In the USA a certain Tari Steward founded the *American Bank Note Company*, which produced notes called «*Million dollar bill*». These notes were manufactured using the identical paper as original American dollars, and had an identical design. However, when it comes to their sale, it is immediately made clear that these are not genuine American currency and that they are not suitable for circulation. They are sold as «great presents for family and friends». On the reverse of these notes was decreed «This certificate is guaranteed only by belief in the American dream»[3].

The exchange rate of government liabilities for goods and services lies behind the value of the real banknotes, an expression of the liability of the government. The value of any monetary unit depends on its buying power[4]. The Harvard University professor H.G. Mankiw defines the value of money as being the amount of goods and services which can be bought with one monetary unit[5]. If an identical object is not secured by the State, it is only worth the sum of its tangible constituent

---

[1] *A.S. Melnikova.* Aforementioned work. Pp. 167, 193.
[2] Ibidem. P. 245.
[3] More details can be found at http:/www.i-a-m.org
[4] *Barr. R.* Aforementioned work. P. 289.
[5] *Mankiw H.G.* Aforementioned work. P. 607.

1,000,000
UNITED STATES OF AMERICA
ONE MILLION DOLLARS
M13123362A
1M
ONE MILLION
SERIES 1988

parts, which is defined by T. Steward, including the additional cost, as 8 US Dollars.

In addition to this it is definitely necessary to note that the overwhelming part of such tangible components of real money is created purely as a defence against forgery and falsification of the liability it expresses and documents. If paper money were not forged this part would be considerably less important.

«In all its abstractness, paper money is «cash in hand» in the sense that it is a visible and tangible material»[1].

A thing possessing natural, useful properties, when divided into two parts, divides its use value. If we take a blank sheet of paper, having as its useful characteristic the possibility of entering onto it a volume of information, and divide it in half, then the use value of the two separate pieces of paper will be approximately half as much. However, if we were to tear a Bank of Russia 10 rouble note in half, it would be an entirely different story. The half without the serial number would not be worth anything, and the other half (with the number) would still have a use value of 10 roubles. Why? Because everyone knows that the Central Bank of the Russian Federation accepts — at their face value — ancient, torn or even charred bank notes if the corresponding serial number is still preserved on them. This example clearly shows that it is necessary for the bank-issuer, when accepting its credits at face value, at least to compare this data with the corresponding serial number of said note in the section «Emissions of money» of the passive part of its balance. Old banknotes are withdrawn from circulation and destroyed by the Central Bank, and the sum total of the Central Bank's obligations, shown in the «Emissions of money» section, is decreased by the sum total of the destroyed banknotes' face value.

Moreover, the word «emission» itself emphasises the obligatory nature of paper money.

The monetary reform in Russia in 1991 is a very interesting example. One «glorious» day, the then Prime Minister Pavlov declared all 50 and 100 rouble notes invalid. On this day, the value of the liability expressed on these notes became equal to zero. These banknotes really just became mere things, and their value became equal to the value of the

---

[1] *Barr. R.* Aforementioned work. P. 288.

paper, ink and typographic services used to produce them. Some of the people who did not manage to exchange their banknotes for the new ones used them to paper the walls of their flats.

Moreover, Article 30 of the Federal Law No. 86-FL «On the Central Bank of the Russian Federation (The Bank of Russia)», of 10th June 2002, states: «**Banknotes and coins are unconditional liabilities of the Bank of Russia and are secured by all its assets** (author's bold — *A.G.*) Banknotes and coins of the Bank of Russia must by law be accepted at their nominal value for all types of payment, for depositing into an account, for investments and for transfer across the whole territory of the Russian Federation.»

The issuer itself decrees directly and unequivocally that its banknotes are a legal liability. So why does the government of the Russian Federation not want to acknowledge such an obvious fact?

By the way, speaking of coins, the given norm clearly decrees that coinage of the Russian Federation is also a liability of the Bank of Russia. In defining its status it is possible to conclude that coinage, like banknotes, **is a State self-addressed bearer bill valid upon presentation with a blank endorsement.** The only difference between coinage and banknotes with the same face value is the liability's material bearer. Banknotes and coins with the same nominal value clearly demonstrate a **unity of content whilst the form varies.**

Later the law describes in detail precisely the obligatory character of money:

«Article 31. Banknotes and coinage of the Bank of Russia cannot be declared void (as having lost power as a legal means of payment), if a sufficiently long transition period is not established to exchange them for the new banknotes and coins. No limitations of any kind in relation to the sum or subject of exchange are permitted.

During the exchange of banknotes and coinage of the Bank of Russia for the new form of tender, the period of withdrawal of banknotes from circulation must be no less than one year, but must not exceed five years.

Article 32. The Bank of Russia **exchanges old worn out banknotes without any limitations** (author's bold — *A.G.*), in accordance with its established rules.

Article 33. The Board of Directors makes the decision about the release into circulation of new banknotes and coinage and about the withdrawal of the old ones, **sets the nominal values** and forms of the new tender. A description of the new tender is released to the public via the media».

Article 4 of this law states: «The Bank of Russia...alone exists as issuer of cash money and organises the circulation of cash.»

And yet again the very concept of «issue» indicates the obligatory character of money. It is not possible to issue tangible objects (fig. 19).

Non-cash currency — deposited money (checking accounts)

Cashless currency arises either as a result of a credit emission, carried out by the central bank of the relevant state, or as the result of a transfer of cash currency in the form of banknotes or coins to a deposit account (a type of savings agreement) (fig. 20).

Deposited money as a form of credit money represents currency in paperless form. From an economic point of view, the existence and development are a result of the following:

• Reducing costs of circulation;
• Speeding up of circulation;
• Practicality and comparative security of cashless transactions;
• Simplicity of supervision of circulation for the State.

This form of money has the following important properties:

1) the side liable to the investor is not the central bank itself, but the private bank in which the funds are accommodated. In turn, the central bank is liable to the private bank. On one hand, storing government banknotes in a private bank, which bears responsibility to the investment only to the extent of its own capital, makes the money less secure in the case of the bankruptcy[1] of the bank. On the other hand, the storing of money in an unsuitable place, for example at home, poses a risk not only to the banknotes themselves, but also to the lives of the owner and his family;

2) this is not a bearer liability, but a nominal one, i.e. it has a property content which a person is not able to hold (*detencio*). In the legal

---
[1] The term «bankruptcy» derives from «bank» and «rupture».

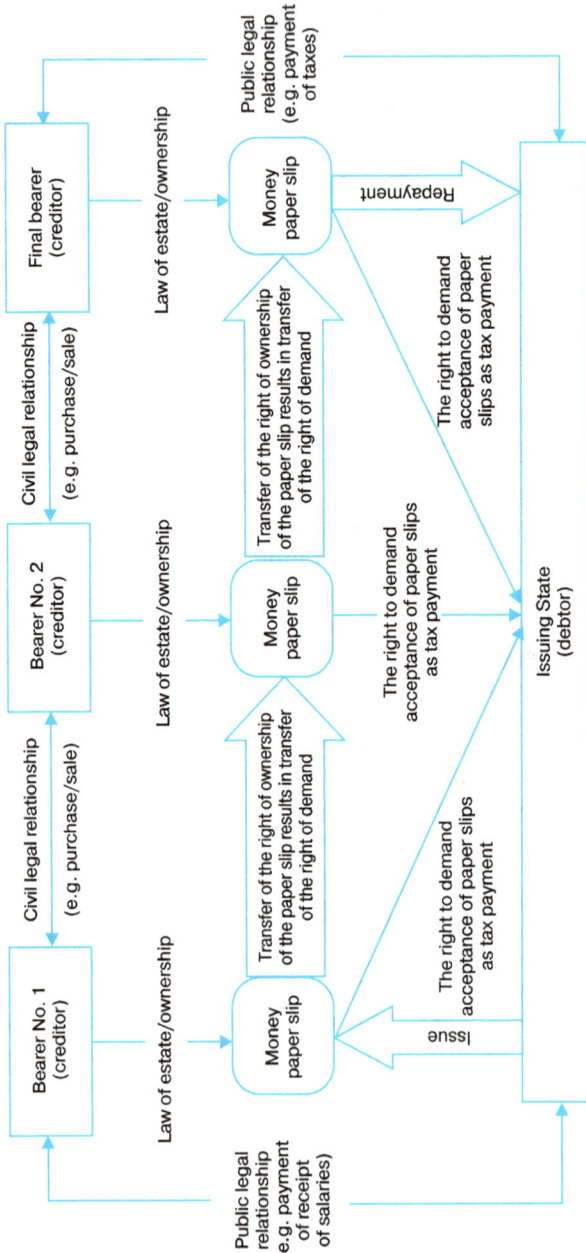

Fig. 19. Circulation of paper currency as a bearer security

Money as a bearer security is a compound security
· Primary right: to demand of the issuer-state to accept paper money slips as tax payment
· Secondary right: ownership of the paper slip
· It is circulated in accordance to secondary legal relations – proprietary

Percentage

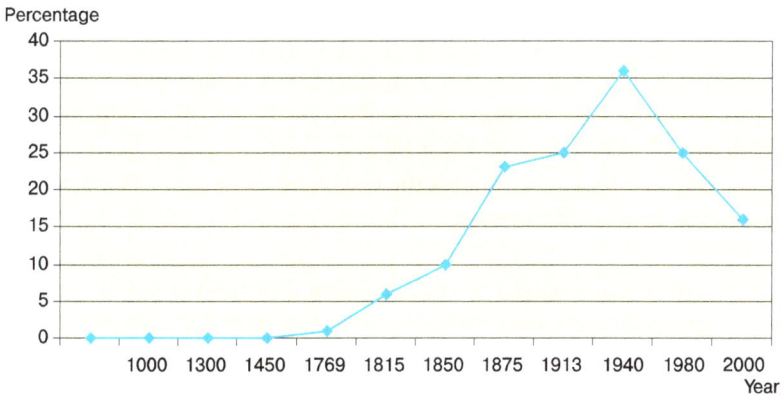

Fig. 20. The share of deposited money

language of the Ancient Romans it would be termed «the right of hold-ing». In addition, the Latin *animus possidenti* (the intention to treat something as one's own) is fully preserved, giving the illusion of owner-ship (*posessio*);

3) the liability becomes dividable by any number with the minimal known discretion, which in turn improves the circulatory function of this form of money.

Deposited money acquired the function of money only with the process of realization of cashless bank accounts i.e. only in the mid 20th century. This became possible only at the time of a corresponding level of development of industrial power, in part thanks to the release of banking mainframes by the company *IBM* and the introduction of *CHIPS*, an electronic system of inter-bank accounts.

L.G. Efimova writes: «In connection with this, economists for a long time did not acknowledge call deposits as being money. When, in 1930, John Maynard Keynes, in his book «Treatise on Money» included call deposit in his concept of money, G. Parker Willis, a famous professor of Colombia University, reacted to this entirely critically[1]. Amongst later economists, practically no opponents to this point of view re-mained[2].

---

[1] *Dolan E. G., Campbell C. D., Campbell R. G.* Money, banking and money-credit policy. Moscow-Leningrad, 1991. P. 40–41.
[2] See, for example: *Samuelson P.* Economics. Vol. 1. Moscow, 1992. P. 258; *Dolan E.G., Campbell C.D., Campbell R. G.* Aforementioned work. P. 32.

According to the French economist Pierre Berger, money is issued by three types of institutions: commercial banks, the state treasury and the issuer bank[1]. In this way, the opinion that the only bank able to issue its money is the Central Bank of the Russian Federation, appears to be erroneous[2][3]. Therefore it is not by chance that Article 29 of the Law on the Bank of Russia stipulates the exclusive right of the Bank of Russia only to emit cash currency.

The problem of the right to issue cashless (credit) money has not been unequivocally solved by the legislator. Insofar as a ban on cashless emissions exists, any commercial bank may issue (and does issue) its money in the form of balances in payment and current accounts. Nobel Prize laureate Friedrich Hayek spoke out in favour of the issue of private money[4]. He proposed that the monetary liability expressed by the currency issued by any concrete issuer would amount to the nominal value. However, different types of currency should be freely exchanged according to the rate of exchange. At the same time F. Hayek spoke out for the necessity for each issuer to support the value (buying power) of his currency in relation to the average set of wholesale products (a standard of price) by means of special, pre-determined measures of influence. «I expect that, at least in wealthy regions, far exceeding present-day national territories, people will be willing to regard an average set of wholesale products as a price standard, in relation to which they would prefer to safeguard the constancy of their money»[5]. Despite scepticism from opponents, Hayek's ideas clearly came to fruition in Russia, where promissory notes of the company «Gazprom» indeed fulfil the function of money, in both wholesale transactions and in the accumulations of financial institutions. The researcher himself suggested that the full realization of his idea requires corresponding political reforms, because governments are unlikely to relinquish the

---

[1] *Berger P.* The money mechanism. Moscow, 1993. P. 21.
[2] The error described above is the result of the instability of legal and economic terms «currency» and «money».
[3] *Efimova L.G.* Can taxes be paid by «dead» money? // *Business and banks*, 1998. Issue 42 (*Ефимова Л.Г.* Возможна ли уплата налогов «мертвыми» деньгами? // *Бизнес и банки*, 1998. № 42).
[4] The term «private money» describes monetary units issued by several competing private (non-State) banks.
[5] *F.A. Hayek.* Private money. Moscow: Institute of the National Economic Model, 1996. P. 126.

profitable privilege of issuing money[1]. However, his idea about private money was partly realized in the form of call deposits.

Some economists and lawyers suggest that such «private monies» do not have a cash/tangible form. Here we are forced to disagree and to point out that «self-addressed» bank bills, issued in exchange for deposits, which are so widespread now in Russia, are in fact «private monies». When such money is termed «private», their private-legal content is implied, in contrast to currency, which has public-legal content.

It is very important to note that their private-legal character applies only in the relationship between the investor and the private bank, whilst the legal relationship between the private bank and the State bank it remains one of a public-legal character.

Thus, deposited money (cashless currency), in the form of balances in the accounts of enterprises and organisations, is money of both the Central Bank of the Russian Federation and of the commercial banks. When a customer withdraws money from his account, then, in essence, one is talking about of the conversion of cashless currency (deposited money) to cash currency, to the banknotes and coinage of the Central Bank of the Russian Federation.

Now we will investigate the legal character of non-cash money. For the purpose of this book, we understand cashless currency as **balances in credit in various client accounts in banks**, to which the application of Chapter 45 of the Civil Code of the Russian Federation extends. They are accounts which are specially intended for carrying out various transactions: payment, current, current currency, correspondence, accounts for the financing of capital investments etc.[2] From a legal point of view, an entry into a bank account serves as a quantitative expression of the legal-liability claim of the client towards the bank. However, this circumstance does not impede the recognition of the bank liabilities as money, taking into account that the latter fulfils the function of a means of payment.

As a liability of the relevant storehouse (bank, depository), cashless money is subject to the law of obligations. An entry into a bank account

---

[1] In this case, «money» means «currency».
[2] It must be noted that Chapter 45 of the CC RF isn't applicable to depo accounts, because not non-cash money, but non-document securities are the basis of such contracts.

attests to what sum (to what measure) the bank is the debtor of its client. In this way, the legal relationship we are examining appears to be relative and arises by the will of each party to the bank account contract. According to this contract, the obligation of the bank consists of the completion of concrete, positive actions. It should carry out the instructions of the client in making payments to a third party, in releasing cash funds to the client within the limits of the balance of his account and likewise it should accept payments owed to the client. The owner of the account's right of demand can be violated above all by the bank, to which the client has the right to lay the same claim[1].

At the present time, the overwhelming majority of money in circulation in Russia is deposited, cashless money, which has almost no tangible expression (discounting the paper receipts on which bank statements are printed). In this way, contemporary deposited cashless money presents itself as a non-document nominal security:

• *for the bank*: dividable State nominal «self-addressed» bills with a blank endorsement in the form of an electronic accounts entry;

• *for the client of the bank*: dividable bank «self-addressed» bills with a blank endorsement in the form of an electronic accounts entry.

When considering the security of such a form of liabilities, we say that the liability of the Central Bank itself is secured, just as in the case of cash currency:

• by the State's obligation to accept it [cashless currency] as payment of taxes;

• by the compulsory acceptance [of cashless currency] as payment for goods and services across the whole territory of the country.

The liability of the private bank should, in theory, be secured by the aforementioned liabilities of the Central Bank, but in the assets of any bank, non-cash currency occupies, in accordance with Basle Principles, no less than 12%, and as a rule, no more than 25%. As a result of the active credit policy of any bank, its liabilities are fundamentally secured by the quality of its credit portfolio.

Despite unity of form, *the means of administration* of money, on the part of the clients, varies from bank to bank, leading to a certain amount of confusion amongst economists.

---

[1] See Chapter 45 of the CC RF.

There is no such thing as «electronic money», but there is an electronic method of gaining access to deposited funds; there is no «plastic money», but there is a method of gaining access to accounts with the help of plastic cards.

We will now introduce the basic methods of the administration of (access to) money:

1. Personal access or by post:
- payment order;
- cheque;
- encashment;

2. Access with the aid of electronic networks:
- retail *e-banking* systems: *SWIFT, CHIPS, FedWire;*
- slips from plastic cards like *VISA*, systems like *CyberCash, Cyberplat;*
- systems like *CheckFree.*

Circulation

This form of money has no consumer value, since it does not exist in tangible form (perhaps it does possess a certain value of joyful emotion, arising when the rich man admires his bank balance, but this is hard to evaluate). The exchange value, as already indicated, depends only on the generally recognized, current reputation of the issuer, and also on the short and long-term expectations of fluctuations of the money in terms of a commodity basket (its buying power).

Since the development of a reliable long-distance communications and computing technology, the banking system was finally able to rid itself of the complex derivative legal relations. This form of money has practically no tangible form.

It is secured against the right to demand its acceptance in payment of taxes and for any payment between two legal parties, with the exception of a relationship known to be retail (not wholesale) commercial. This exception, of accepting cash currency as payment for goods, is conditionally licensed by the government in order to support a steady demand for non-cash currency.

Demand for currency

Besides generally known factors of demand for money, including those described by Keynes and Friedman, demand for cash and non-cash currency not guaranteed by gold, forms as a result of the following factors, which, rather than being of economic character, are of a precisely juridical, public-legal nature.

1. The necessity of paying taxes. Any upstanding government accepts only its own currency as payment of taxes. Correspondingly, the demand for currency depends on:

- The capabilities of said government to collect taxes;
- The ability of the economy of said government to produce taxable grounds, for example, taxable additional cost and taxable preservation of property;
- Desire and capability of tax-payers to pay taxes.

However, it is sufficiently obvious that high rates of taxation lead to the flight of industry to other jurisdictions, and low rates of taxation lead to weakening of the government's ability to defend its borders and to maintain order within the sovereign territory. Tax rate in the USA is the main publicly discussed issue and fluctuates, depending on the condition of the economy and the general public will, in the region of 20–30%.

2. The necessity of transactions with the State for the purchase of State property. This is not an overly important factor, which actually works in the case of the privatisation by the government of wealthy enterprises.

3. The necessity of having precisely State-supported means of paying any debt or making any payment within the territory of said State. This issue arises particularly sharply with the significant risk of disputes emerging when deals (transactions) are being made. If there is sufficient faith in the judicial resolution of a conflict, settlement of a debt with an improper means of payment can be a serious argument against the payer. But this factor directly depends on the strength of the government. In periods of discord and change of government, the aforementioned factor works against the currency or in favour of such private-legal liabilities, like bills/promissory notes or bank liabilities or in favour of natural commodity money.

4. The demand for currency for hoarding purposes, arising as a result of a lower level of faith in the government, compared to other issuers. This emerges usually in the case when confidence in one's own government or in its ability to keep inflation in check, is essentially lower than confidence in other governments. An example of this is the Russians' total lack of confidence in the Russian rouble as a means of stabilising prices, arising in part as a result of Pavlov's reforms, which withdrew 50 and 100 rouble banknotes from circulation without compensation, and also as a result of many years of inflation and hyperinflation, which had regularly cheapened cash and non-cash currency. The author is personally acquainted with people who had invested 10,000 roubles in Sberbank in the 1980s, which at that time was enough to buy a «Volga» car or a decent house, and now is enough only to buy a children's bike.

5. The demand for currency for hoarding purposes, arising as a result of confidence in a government which capably supports a reliable and functional banking system. For example, the total collapse of the banking system in 1998 does not facilitate long-term storage of money, in the form of long-term rouble deposits.

A series of experts (the author included) believe that the fundamental causes of bank crises are not so much the sharp fluctuations in property prices (for building societies), in share prices (for investment banks), currency etc., as much as the incorrect fulfilment by the government of its regulatory function, which involves not allowing the warping of the credit portfolios of banks in one or another branch of the economy. For example, in the USA after the crisis of 1930–1933 banks were prohibited by legislation from acquiring shares.

6. Convenient currency legislation. If the government prohibits the circulation of its own currency abroad, it is difficult for it to hope that foreign citizens and businesses will accumulate this currency.

Financial money

Here we should consider:

1) highly liquid assets, for which only insignificant fluctuations in value are possible and which are termed «almost money»

2) stocks and shares (securities), which partially fulfil the functions of money.

Quasi–money

Quasi-money (from the Latin *quasi* — as if) is the name for the monetary means represented by fixed term and savings investments (in commercial banks, special credit institutions), deposit certificates, State treasury liabilities etc. (Fig. 21)

Percentage

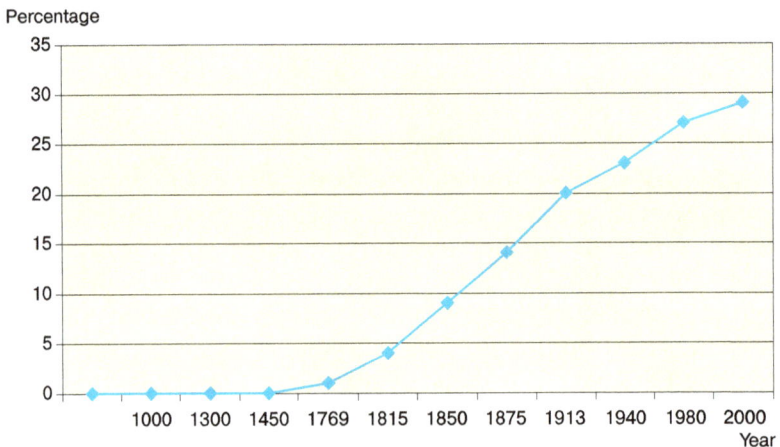

Fig. 21. Prevalence of quasi-money

In order to define the ease with which any type of assets can be turned into an economically-viable medium of circulation, economists use the term «liquidity». As money fulfils the economic role of a means of circulation, it is the most liquid type of asset. The liquidity of other assets can vary. The majority of organisations, at any moment, can be sold with minimal transaction costs and fluctuations in share prices; therefore they serve as relatively liquid assets. «It is only the likeness of money, since it is not possible to use them directly as a means of buying and paying. In the conditions of contemporary capitalism, quasi-money is the main and the most dynamic component of monetary aggregates»[1].

Many economists emphasise such a factor as liquidity when answering the given question. From their point of view, any product which can be turned very quickly into money, can be included in the monetary mass.

On the one hand, it is a highly practical and simple model for discussion, allowing us to regard as aggregate M1 precious metals and other goods, which can be turned into money on the goods market in the twinkling of an eye. But then the question arises: what period of liquidity does a product have to have, in order for it to be included in the monetary aggregate? And if such a period is equals one day, then why not include in the M1 aggregate those market goods which become money in the course of a market session, such as metals, cereals, oil, concentrated orange juice? And what about a studio apartment in Moscow with a one-day period of liquidity?

Stocks and shares, partially fulfilling the functions of money

As we have already elucidated, in order to consider any product as money, it is necessary to prove that it fulfils the functions of money.

Securities, depending on their type, can, in suitable conditions, fulfil all the functions of money to some degree (fig. 22):

• there exists a widespread practice of mortgaging securities (principally corporate shares) as a guarantee when taking a loan. Thus, mortgaged securities fulfil the function of money, serving as a measure of value. Moreover, market estimates of corporate shares reflect the value of the company;

• during mega deals, involving acquisitions of companies in the USA, transactions are usually carried out with the shares of the company-absorber (parent company), which serve as the means of payment[2].

---

[1] *L.N. Krasavina.* Currency and credit under capitalism. Moscow, 1980. P. 126 (*Краса-вина Л.Н.* Денежное обращение и кредит при капитализме. М., 1980. С. 126).

[2] Inevitably, a question arises about the number of people who accept this or that type of money as a means of payment. This number can be either enormous — billions of users in case of the US dollar in cash form, or tiny — about 100 users in case of the Yap island

Percentage

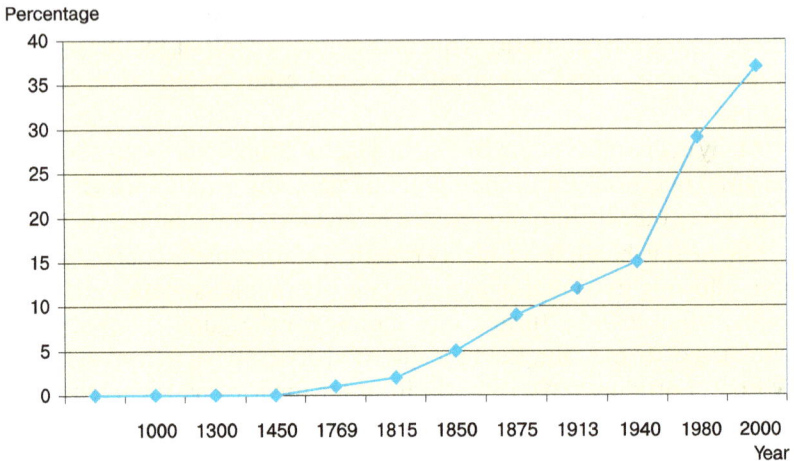

Fig. 22. Prevalence of securities

Equally, company shares, estimated on the market, sometimes fulfil the function of circulation during the resolution of disputes. For example, on the 10th of August 2004, the company *Yahoo!* agreed to drop its patent lawsuit against *Google*, in exchange for 2.7 million shares in the latter[1];

• the intended purpose of such a security as a bank cheque is exactly one of the functions of money: to serve as a means of payment;

• the direct intended purpose of deposit certificates is to serve a means of accumulation;

• a bill/promissory note can fulfil the function of a means of payment (if the issuer issues it together with a payment of some monetary sum at the time of a deal of one kind or another), the function of a means of saving/accumulation owing to a discount and the function of a means of circulation. Well-known issuers, such as the company «Gazprom», fulfill the last function.

Let us consider a concrete example: cheques.

According to Article 877 of the Civil Code of the Russian Federation «a cheque is recognised as a security, containing an unconditional in-

_____

stone money. Definition of the sufficient number of users is a massive undertaking, which deserves to become a separate piece of research.

[1] http://www.inline.ru/internet.asp?NewsID=46541 (Credit: *The Washington Post*).

struction by the cheque-giver to the bank, to make a payment of the sum specified on the cheque to the cheque-bearer.»

From the point of view of legislation, transactions made by cheque are just as common as transactions made by payment order. It is obvious that cheques fulfil the function of a means of payment and a means of circulation. Their measure of worth is reflected by the sum inscribed on the cheque. However, the function of saving/accumulation is essentially reduced in a cheque, insofar as it is valid for a relatively short period of time. Although, one must acknowledge that 20–30-year old banknotes also become invalid in a number of countries.

The following example is Minfin bonds, known in Russia as «OGV-VZ» (Obligations of the State Inner Currency Loan).

It is obvious that they fulfil the function of a means of payment, although not in a very wide sector. The main ideologue, which attaches the payment function to «OGVVZ», was and remains the Russian Ministry of Finance (Minfin), which offers the possibility to use Minfin bonds for clearing a debt, buying debts of foreign governments, carrying out mutual tax-related settlements and regulating/classifying payments.

In transactions between Russian parent companies and their subsidiaries abroad Minfin bonds are used extremely often as a means of circulation and even as international currency. Often they are used as a means of giving credit to subsidiaries abroad. It is necessary to note that, in contrast to the use of local currency, the use of securities as a means of payment requires the agreement of the receiver (beneficiary).

A means of accumulation easily manifests itself theoretically by the very nature of a bond as a means of saving, and practically, via the analysis of fund portfolios of banks, insurance companies and various funds, which are the most active investors into Minfin bonds.

The measure of value is reflected by the document's face value and its market rate.

Generally speaking, we are concluding that if one or another security fulfils the function of money, then it is possible to recognize it as money.

In economics, there are many things of which it is impossible to talk in precise terms.

For example, do types of money such as coins actually fulfil the function of money, in super-wholesale transactions of 1 billion roubles (33 million US Dollars)[1] and over? No, they do not. Does this mean that coins are not money? Things are not at all simple. It is not possible to describe one type of money with 100% certainty as *ideally* fulfilling the function of money, because:

- non-cash money is impractical for small transactions;
- cash is impractical in the case of a delayed shipment of goods, where a letter of credit would be more convenient;
- in remote regions payment in commodities (vodka, ammunition etc.) is preferred;
- transactions involving company acquisitions and mergers are often paid for by shares of the acquirer-company.

Not one type of money ideally fulfils the function of money; each type of money is convenient in one or another situation (fig. 23).

For example, coins serve the sector of transactions well, when the sum to be paid does not exceed the value of the 10 highest denominations of coins, and, in case of banknotes, when the sum to be paid does not exceed the 300 highest denominations of currency. In relation to bigger deals, cashless methods of payment are more convenient. In a cash-orientated economy, it is not unheard of for expensive property to be bought with cash, but this is moving away from the area of the theory of money, and more a case of the theory of efficient taxation.

Thus, some shares also fulfil the function of money, but not ideally, and they are only used in some sectors of economics. For example, bills/promissory notes of the Russian companies «Gazprom» and «Sberbank RF» were widely accepted as payment during real, high-pressure deals for metal and metal products in the regions.

---

[1] Rouble to US Dollar exchange rate is given at the time this research was carried out.

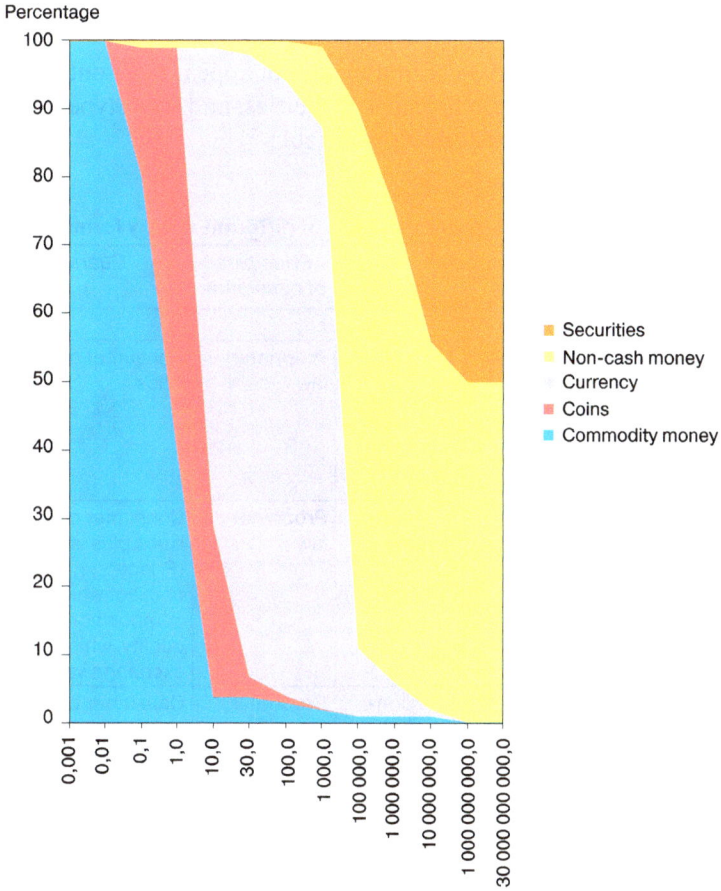

Fig. 23. The convenience of circulation of the various types of money

Object and liability components of money

The physical properties of money do not appear as essential. Money does not have common physical properties, and some types of money do not even have a material form. (table 7)

Table 7
Object and liability components of different money forms

Form of money	Component, %		Principles of circulation	Guarantee
	Object	*Liability*		
Natural				
Non-standard-ized goods e.g. skins, salt, crops, metals by weight (commodity)	100	0	Proprietary law	Consumer character-istics
Stamped metal ingots of precise weight, stamped «kunas»	95	1 — con-sumer 5 — ex-change	Proprietary law	Consumer character-istics plus issuer's (Prince's) guarantee of exact weight, composition and quality, which added to exchange value
Coins made of precious metals	90	2 — con-sumer 10 — ex-change	Proprietary law	Consumer character-istics, plus responsi-bility of manufacturer-issuer (Prince) for exact weight and composition, which added to exchange value
Credit				
Commercial bills	0.1	99.9	Law of obligations for regis-tered bills, proprietary law for bearer bills in circula-tion.	Obligation of the issuer (merchant, industrialist) to issue value indicated (in gold, coins, goods) was guaranteed by his property and earning potential.

Table 7 cont.

Form of money	Component, %		Principles of circulation	Guarantee
	Object	Liability		
Banknotes from private banks	0.1	99.9	Law of obligations for issue and encashment, proprietary law for circulation	Liability of a private bank to issue gold, coinage etc was secured by its assets
State banknotes (T-notes):	1	99	Law of obligations for issue and encashment, proprietary law for circulation	Liability of the State bank to issue gold, coinage etc is guaranteed by its assets, the State's property, the right of the State to collect taxes
with metal «guarantee»				Liability of the State bank to issue gold, coinage etc is guaranteed by its assets, the State's property, the right of the State to collect taxes, by the liability of the government to accept currency X as payment for taxes and the clearing of State credits
Without metal «guarantee»				The abstract liability of the State bank is secured by the liability of the government to accept currency X as payment for taxes and the clearing of State credits
Coins with face value (the stage of transition to credit money)	5–70, depending on a coin's composition	30–95 depending on a coin's composition	Law of obligations for issue and encashment, proprietary law for circulation	Consumer characteristics plus liability of manufacturer-issuer (Prince), which was secured by his property, his right to collect taxes and to lead aggressive wars

End of table 7

Form of money	Component, %		Principles	Guarantee
	Object	Liability	of circulation	
Deposited money (checking accounts)	0.01	99.9	Law of obligations	Same as above, but divided, nominal and, as a rule, from a private bank
Financial				
Quasi-money	0.01–0.1	99.9–99.99	Law of obligations	The abstract liability of the financial institution to issue, within the period specified, currency, either in cash or cashless form, was guaranteed either by the right of the government to collect taxes or by the credit portfolio of the bank
Stocks and shares, partially fulfilling the functions of money	0.01–0.1	99.9–99.99	Law of obligations	Share is guaranteed by the competence of the shareholder; bonds — by the right to demand payment, in case of other securities — other rights were guaranteed by the issuer's property and earning potential

It is essential to note that precise calculations of the object and liability components of different types of money are only possible with concrete examples.

For example, if the cost of manufacturing US Dollar banknotes equals 50 cents, then the object component value of one-dollar coin will equal 50%, and in 100 dollars it will be 0.5. Equally, when attempting to define the object component of non-cash currency, it is possible to carry out the following calculation: information about the name of the owner of the account and the state of his bank balance occupies no more than 40 bytes. A hard disc with a capacity of 40 gigabytes nowadays costs no more than 100 dollars. Therefore, the cost of storing such information is 10^{-7} dollars. If a certain account-holder only has 1 dollar in his account, then the object component will equal 10^{-5} and if he has 1 billion dollars, then the object component will equal 10^{-14} %.

Yu. Maltsev and I. Shkarinov write: «The legislator calls money an object **only because of the convenience and expediency of regulating the legal relations linked to owning and managing money in accordance with proprietary law, although in essence these relations are ones of obligatory/liability nature.**

...The consumer value of money lies in the fact that it serves as a general equivalent, mediating the exchange of all other property. Its economic character of general equivalent has not yet been reflected by the law and is the cause of misunderstandings, which the formation of purely legal constructions leads us to... In fact, insofar as it is impossible to effectively apply methods of defence (vindicatory and negatory lawsuits), characteristic of the law of estate/proprietary law, to the demand for cash, then the status of money as some sort of material object loses its meaning»[1].

Table 8

Legal relations, arising during the use of different money forms

Form of money	Legal relationship	
	Primary	*Secondary*
Non-standardized goods e.g. skins, salt, crops, metals by weight (commodity)	The right of ownership and other proprietary rights	–
Stamped metal ingots of precise weight, stamped «kunas»	The right of ownership and other proprietary rights, the right to demand exchange for the specified amount of gold	–
Precious metal coins	The right of ownership and other proprietary rights, the right to demand exchange for the specified amount of gold	–
Commercial bills: Registered/Nominal	Unconditional abstract liability of the tradesman to	

---

[1] *Maltsev Yu., Shkarinov I.* On the problem of guarantee-free indisputable money withdrawing from banks' correspondent accounts // *Business and banks*, 1996. Issues 22–23 (*Мальцев Ю., Шкаринов И.* К проблеме безакцептного и бесспорного списания денежных средств с корсчетов банков // *Бизнес и банки*, 1996. № 22–23).

Table 8 cont.

Form of money	Legal relationship	
	Primary	Secondary
Bearer	pay the intended party within the intended period the specified amount of certain precious metals The right of ownership of the paper slip with inscription	Unconditional abstract liability of the tradesman to pay the intended party within the intended period the specified amount of certain precious metals
Banknotes from private banks	The right of ownership of the paper slip of the banknote	Unconditional abstract liability of the tradesman to pay the intended party within the intended period the specified amount of certain precious metals or precious metal coins
State banknotes (T-notes):		
with metal «guarantee»	The right of ownership of the paper slip of the banknote The public right to use this banknote to make *any* payment within the borders of the country	Unconditional abstract liability of the tradesman to pay the intended party within the intended period the specified amount of certain precious metals or precious metal coins, unconditional abstract right of presentation as a means of settling any transactions with the State.
without metal «guarantee»	The right of ownership of the paper slip of the banknote The public right to use this banknote to make *any* payment within the borders of the country (now it is limited in comparison with deposited money)	Unconditional abstract right of presentation as a means of settling any transactions with the State.

Form of money	Legal relationship	
	Primary	Secondary
Coins with face value (the stage of transition to credit money)	The right of ownership of the metal bearer, the public right to use this banknote to make *any* payment within the borders of the country (now it is limited in comparison with deposited money)	Unconditional abstract right of presentation as a means of settling any transactions with the State
Deposited money (checking accounts)	The right to demand from the bank to issue cash currency / make a specified payment, public right to accept this money for *any* transaction within the borders of the country (with the exception of retail)	–
Quasi-money	Private-legal right to demand payment of deposited money from a bank or the Treasury within a specified period	–
Shares and other proprietary rights	Rights of the shareholder or other stock rights	–

Having analysed the forms of money, we obtain a graph of their proportional prevalence at different times (fig. 24).

From fig. 24, we can conclude that, with the development of civil and industrial relations, the demand for exchange value of money is higher than for its direct consumer value.

However, during an industrial crisis and the resulting crisis of public confidence in the national currency, a reverse process takes place, when all those involved in the circulation of goods, expecting to go completely bankrupt, try to convert exchange value into consumer value. In this way, a society's turning away from one form of money during a time of crisis bears witness to the fact that this type of money has lost the function of money and therefore is being ousted from monetary circulation. Up until the crisis it was regarded as money, but during and after the crisis it is simply no longer accepted.

However, in case of normal development, the object component/ value of different forms of money strives towards zero, since an im-

Percentage

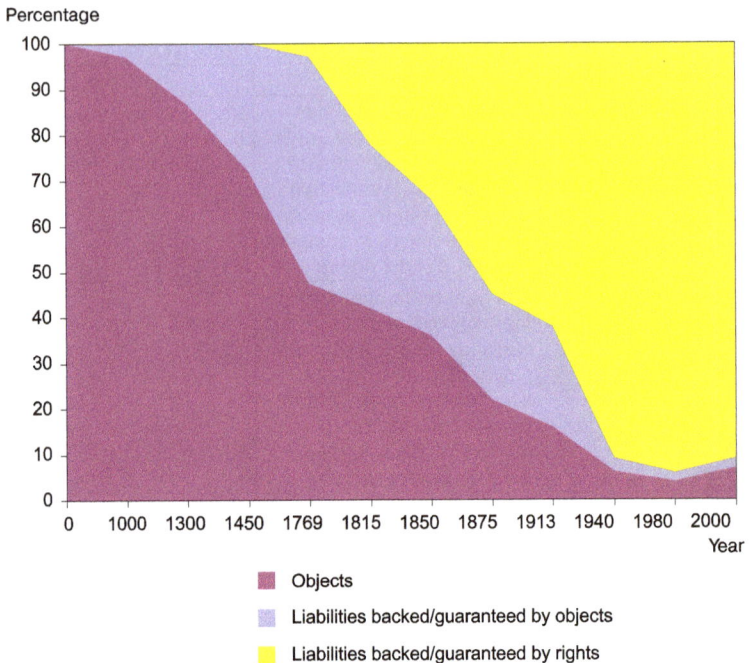

Fig. 24. Share of different money forms

provement in the circulation of money leads to reducing representation of liability information in object form. We can illustrate this with the following example.

In Ancient Babylon liabilities (promissory notes) were written on stone tablets weighing up to a kilogram, in Ancient Rome they were written on clay tablets weighing up to 300 grams. After that the bearer of such information became a parchment with a weight of 100 grams, from the fifteenth century onwards it became paper (10g) and nowadays the information is carried nearly everywhere on electronic bearers, where one liability occupies approximately 100 thousand molecules of silicon: much less than 1 mg. Bill Gates' development of electronic technology and «the reduction of the co-efficient of information friction»[1] with the creation of the quantum computer will reduce the electronic bearer to between 10 and 100 atoms.

[1] *Gates B.* The road into the future. Moscow, 1997. P. 20

Now the value of a product is fully separated from its physical form and appears in a distinct, public form, without the need to be attached to some or other type of material commodity body. It represents a public symbol of a physical commodity and functions in the same vein, relying only on public guarantee. Its value now is expressed simply by a number, confidence in which is confirmed by the agreement of separate parties, and also by the agreement of the public and the government. The latter guarantees this confidence in the name of the public and on the basis of the power invested in it by the people, by means of the corresponding legislation and established procedures.

Thus, the public role of money, as a representative of value, signifies that every type of commercial money is full-bodied money, regardless of whether or not it has a physical content. **Whether money is full-bodied is defined not by its existence in a purely material form, but by its ability to completely fulfil the functions dictated by the demands of the corresponding stage of commercial relations development[1].**

---

[1] *Portnoy M.A.* Aforementioned work. P. 27.

Analysis of the movement of money forms

Turning to the analysis of Article 128 of the Civil Code of the Russian Federation, we will move away from the fact that the following arises from the economic nature of money: **it is not possible to talk about the legal nature of money in general.** It is only possible to talk about the legal nature and corresponding **legal regime of a concrete type of legal property goods, which carries out the function of money**[1].

By analysing the table of the forms of money (see table 3), the table of the material and liability content of different forms of money (see table 7) and also the corresponding graphs, it is possible to come to the conclusion there is an evolutionary ousting of one form of money by another more suited to the corresponding level of industrial relations and in contemporary economics literally all types of money exist, having, however, varying degrees of prevalence in economic relations.

Likewise it is necessary to point out, in accordance with M.A. Portnoy, that different forms of money have different abilities to fulfil the functions of money. For example, banknotes are an inadequate means of preserving value (accumulation), nominal credit bills are not quite suitable as a means of circulation, and financial money is inadequate both as a means of circulation and as a means of payment. At the same time, all of these are adequate as a measure of value[2].

It is particularly worth noting the following tendencies:

* absolute majority of contemporary money forms are of liability character;
* financial money is at present the most actively developing form of money;
* the development of electronic systems of access to deposited and financial money (*e-banking* and *e-trading* systems) allow fund-holders to reduce «inactive» sums of deposited money by means of short term investment in stock and shares, which exerts essential influence on the global liquidity of the international system as a whole.

---

1 *Efimova L.G.* Is tax payment by «dead» money a possibility? // *Business and banks*, 1998. Issue 42 (*Ефимова Л.Г.* Возможна ли уплата налогов «мертвыми» деньгами? // *Бизнес и банки*, 1998. № 42).
2 See: *Portnoy M.A.* Aforementioned work. P. 164.

- the spiral development of history exemplifies the fact that mankind, having become acquainted with «portfolio» distribution of stock and shares into different branches of economics for increased stability, has created stable «portfolio» deposited money (*SDR, ECU)* and even banknotes (*EURO)*;
- the development of commercial markets and electronic systems of accessing natural products markets, and likewise the use of the «liquidity line» as a mechanism distinctive to deposited money, in the sector of contracts relating to stocks and shares, allows investment funds to retain an essential part of their assets in exchange traded commodities (ETCs), such as of oil products, light and dark metals and even concentrated orange juice, which again endows commodity money with the function of accumulation (fig. 25).

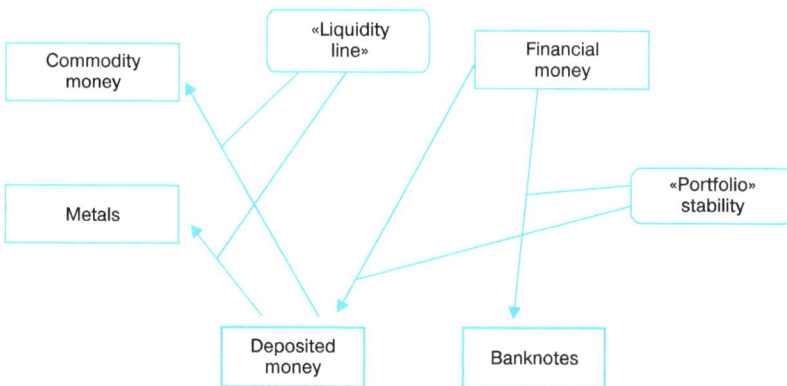

Fig. 25. The expansion of the sphere of application
of specific functions of money

The signing of international deals, such as, for example, «oil for supply of provisions» between Iraq and the international community, the acquisition of Russian credits by Iraq with oil and oil products; «gifts» in the form of trains full of oil products to government officials of several developing countries — finds us drawing a conclusion that a certain tendency has taken shape, i.e. certain ETCs are acquiring the function of circulation and, consequently, developing into money.

Such ETCs in circulation take the following forms:
- nominal securities in the form of storage receipts, bills of lading;
- bearer securities in the form of bearer storage receipts, bills of lading «upon presentation»;
- «metal» and other commodity accounts, arising as a result of the storage of goods in special depositories. The Canadian company «Kitco» is the best-known of such depositories of precious metals, which gives its clients the right to carry out non-cash operations between themselves. Equally well-known is non-cash circulation of such goods and rights for them on various commodity exchanges in the West, amongst which the Chicago goods exchange and London's metal exchange stand out for their popularity and volume of trade.

Thus, it is possible to establish that the historical spiral development of forms of money results in all types of existing money advancing to a new level.

At present, forms of money which are of a liability nature, serve the overwhelming majority of deals. Applying to them object/material rules of circulation is not only unacceptable, but also creates huge problems in the circulation of money, and consequently negatively affects the credit-monetary system and the development of economics as a whole.

Many lawyers confirm, that one or another form of money inadequately fulfils one or another function of money. In particular, there is much criticism of the fulfilment of the function of payment by securities. Here we once again emphasise that not one form of money ideally fulfils any one function (table 9).

Table 9
Fulfilment of the money functions by different forms of money in Russia

Form of money	Percentage of function fulfilment		
	Measure of value	Means of circulation and payment	Means of accumulation (value preservation), holders
Natural			
Non-standardized goods e.g. skins, salt, crops, metals by weight (commodity)	2	0	100–120 Property for rent, building materials, cars, flats, (B, PF, IC, IF, physical persons)

Table 9 cont.

Form of money	Percentage of function fulfilment		
	Measure of value	*Means of circulation and payment*	*Means of accumulation (value preservation), holders*
Stamped metal ingots of precise weight	0.1	3 Barter is especially well-developed in the coal sector (coal for metal)	100 Oil, non-ferrous and ferrous metals (enterprises which use them as raw materials, IF)
Precious metal coins	0.1	0.1	110 Value increases with time (for numismatists)
Credit			
Commercial bills	20	10 In payments for metal	110 (B, PF, IC, IF)
Banknotes from private banks	20	10 During receipt of wholesale goods from factories in the regions	85 Risk of bankruptcy + inflation (B, PF, IC)
State banknotes (T-notes) without metal «guarantee»	50	50 Prohibited from use at above the defined limit between juridical persons (practically prohibited from circulation in wholesale trade). Only short-term liquidity: routine payments, due taxes	90 in case of 10% inflation 10–20 in case of hyperinflation
Deposited money (checking accounts)	60	90 Circulates poorly in the retail sector, Except credit cards	90

End of table 9

Form of money		Percentage of function fulfilment		
		Measure of value	*Means of circulation and payment*	*Means of accumulation (value preservation), holders*
US Dollars	Banknotes	99 The best price currency in all (both domestic and foreign) contracts	25 The black market, property, between physical persons, since the government prohibits their circulation	97 In case of inflation of 3% (with the exception of the 1970–1973 crisis)
	Deposited	99	10 shadow payments for wholesale trade and property	97
Financial				
Quasi-money		1	0.1	99 Percentage of income almost equals inflation (B, PF, IC, IF)
Shares and other property rights		1	0.1	120–150 Profitability of normal business (related enterprises, colleagues, physical persons)

Key: B = banks, PF = pension funds, IC = insurance companies, IF = investment funds.

Part IV
MISTAKES IN LEGISLATION AND THE ROLE OF ECONOMIC THEORY

The origin of mistakes

> *In terms of law only material objects are recognised as things.*
>
> The German Civil Code, § 90

A mistake relating to the nature of money in Russian civil legislation arose because of the fact that Roman law was taken as its basis, without considering the new tendencies in monetary circulation and the monetary system.

In actual fact, in Ancient Rome only object acted as money: metals (copper, silver, gold), because, at that level of trade relations, promissory notes, bills and assignations were not in circulation.

Life has changed substantially since the time of Ancient Rome. Naturally, evolution has also touched the sphere of money. However, contemporary legislators, having revived Roman law in the Civil Code of the Russian Federation, have not taken into account the fact that metal ceased to fulfil the function of a measure of value long time ago, and that deals are no longer conducted with the need for a weighman with scales and weights.

It is possible that the said mistake was a result of an unfaithful translation from Latin, insofar as the Latin word «res» had the two following meanings:

1) a separate, legally independent material entity with clear spatial boundaries;

2) any object (including intangibles — *jura*) of private law or the civil process (*ausa*), and also a whole complex of assets (*bona, hereditas; patrimonium*)[1].

Gaius[2] thus divides things into tangible (*corporals*), which it is possible to feel or touch (*quae tangi possunt*) and intangible (*incorporales*) which it is not possible to feel or touch (*quae tangi non possunt*). Gaius interprets the latter not as things in the sense of objects of the external world, but precisely as rights[3]. «Intangibles are things which cannot be touched, including those which are listed in the law, such as inheritance, usufruct, liabilities, whatever their form, and the fact that inheritance includes physical items is not at all important... nor the fact that a large part of what is left to us, according to some sort of liability, is a physical object... but the law of inheritance itself, the law of usufruct, liability law are all regarded as *res incorporales,* i.e. intangible objects»[4] (Gai.2.14) This fragment is also reproduced literally in Digests[5] (D.1.8.1)

Contemporary Russian law, however, recognises under the concept of «a thing» only objects of the material world, which exist in their natural condition in nature or are created by the labour of man[6].

As N.O. Nersesov explained, «references to **Roman law** (in this case — *A.G.*) are out of place because securities are essentially a product of the cultural life of new peoples, and consequently, it is not possible to attach to them new norms which are taken from a law foreign to them, Roman law. The latter **is of historical interest to present day society** and serves as a excellent school for the training of lawyers, **but it is impossible to find the answers in it to all questions, occurring in the lives of other nations, at any time»** [7].

---

[1] *Bartosek M.* Roman law (notions, terms, definitions): Translated from Czech. Moscow, 1989. P. 274 (*Бартошек М.* Римское право (понятия, термины, определения): Пер. с чешск. М., 1989. С. 274).
[2] A famous Roman lawyer, a recognised figure of authority in Ancient Roman law.
[3] Roman private law: Textbook / Edited by Prof. Novitsky I.B. and Prof. Peretersky I.S. Moscow, 1996. P. 148.
[4] *Gaius.* Institutes. Books 1–4. Moscow, 1997.
[5] Justinian Digests. Selected excerpts. Moscow: Nauka, 1984.
[6] *Baskakova M.A.* Businessman's Juridical Dictionary / Edited by Ryasentsev V.A. Moscow, 1994. P. 77 (*Баскакова М.А.* Толковый юридический словарь бизнесмена / Научн. ред. В.А. Рясенцев. М., 1994. С. 77).
[7] *N.O. Nersesov.* Representation and securities in civil law. Moscow, 1998. P. 18 (*Нерсесов Н.О.* Представительство и ценные бумаги в гражданском праве. М.: Статут, 1998. С. 18).

«The majority of lawyers, who are examining contemporary legal phenomena chiefly from the point of view of Roman law, achieve unsatisfactory results which are unrelated to the demands of real life»[1]. N.O. Nersesov renders this statement concrete with the example of the negative influence of Roman law on the development of commodity circulation with the help of bearer securities in France.

«The convenience of the examined form of liability in relation to facilitating the concession of rights of demand became hindered by the gradual development of theoretical jurisprudence. The history of the development of juridical thought in France at that time without doubt took place under the strong influence of Roman law.

In their explanations of the different institutions of civil law, lawyers increasingly relied on Roman law. The latter, called *droit commun* as early as in the 13ᵗʰ century by a lawyer *Beaumenoir*, as time passed, became in the eyes of lawyers, educated under its exclusive influence, the higher law, *autorite*.

The influence of Roman law unprofitably affected the theoretical basis of imperfect bearer securities. As a product of the general law of France, these liabilities did not suit the strict demands of Roman contract law. Intricate analysis of juridical concepts was alien to the juridical genius of the 13ᵗʰ-century French; the common sense of the people, having revealed itself in the fragmentary opinions of a small number of professional lawyers of the time and also in juridical practices, considered the bearer (porteur de lettre) as an independent creditor in relation to the promissory document.

Meanwhile, later lawyers, with a better theoretical training, came to apply the Roman theory of mandate to the bearer, the owner of the document. Such a transition, incidentally, was completed gradually. Thus, a 15ᵗʰ-century lawyer *Ioannes Gallus*, although considering the bearer *(porteur)* to be the mandatary, maintains that his right according to the document did not end with the death of the trustee.

Someone who talks in particular detail about these liabilities is the 16ᵗʰ-century lawyer *Rebuffus*, who tries to reconcile the theory of mandate with the independent juridical situation of the owner, by means of supposition (presumption). In his opinion, the bearer always has the

---

[1] Ibidem. P. 199.

right to file a claim on the strength of the supposition that the document came to him as a deed of trust; to this he attaches another basis, that the debtor cannot raise any kind of objection since he has himself promised to make a payment to any bearer.

As a result, triumphant once and for all was the point of view of Roman law, i.e. that the bearer is only an implementer of the rights of another party, the original creditor, and therefore he should have presented either a power of attorney, if he was acting in the name of the principal, or a proof of a completed procedure of *cessio bonorum*, if he was acting in his own name.

This point of view is reflected in the later versions of coutumes (*Translator's note*: bodies of law in force in France until the Revolution) composed undoubtedly under the influence of lawyers educated in theory. The coutumes of Orleans appear, to a certain extent, to be an exception. In the first edition (1509), chapter XXI, *Des executions faites par vertu de letters obligatoires etc., art. 348*, there is a mention of the *«porteur de letters obligatoires»* (bearer) who can act in relation to the debtor as if he were an independent creditor. This article remained without alteration even in the revised edition of 1583, only in a different part of the document, precisely in chapter XX, *art. 432*.

From the article mentioned it appears that the *porteur* (bearer) is more independent than the ordinary commissioner. This particularly stands out in the second half of the article, where it is said that the bearer may continue the legal suit (of calling the debtor to account) even after the death of the creditor.

We note here that one of the contemporary French lawyers, *Amedée Pétit*, basing himself on the abovementioned article 432 of the coutumes of Orleans (the 1583 edition), finds that, at that time, *genuine bearer securities* have already been known. In this he refers to the authority of Potier. In fact this academic explains the phrase in art. 432 *«si a ce ledit debteur est oblige»* in the sense that the debtor pledged by agreement to pay the bearer, and to this adds that in commercial dealings these bills *«sont encore autorises»*. The opinion of Potier is refuted by the second half of the same phrase, *«comme seroit (porteur) le creancier principal»*, from which it is directly clear that an imperfect form of bearer liability is being discussed, examples of which we included above, i.e. where the debtor is liable to pay a defined, original creditor or a bearer of the document.

The bearer of the document (*porteur de lettres obligatoires*) had the character of a legal representative, which is clear from comparison with other similar statements of the coutumes. Thus, in the coutumes *de Montargis* of 1531, in chapter XX, «*d'executions de letters obligatoires*», the content of art. 432 of the coutumes of Orleans is repeated and the following 26th article states that «*lettres obligatoires*» cannot be brought into use by the bearer after the death of the creditor and that heirs of the latter may have a claim against the debtor.

From the fact, that the right of the bearer to pursue a claim against the debtor is cut short by the death of the creditor, it is clear that such a bearer is only regarded as an entrusted party, who is acting in the name of the principal, original creditor.

In the coutumes *de Blois* of 1523, chapter XXIII, *art. 250*, the same is repeated. In his notes on this article, the 16th-century lawyer *Julien Brodeau* states that the «*porteur de lettres obligatoires*» is an ordinary trustee (*procurer*).

Thus, **bearer liabilities**, which, according to the development of civil relations, should have turned out to be convenient because of facilitated transferral of rights of demand, on the contrary, **lost their original meaning in the 16th century under the influence of lawyers, inspired by Roman law,** and, as a result, at that time they did not differ substantially from simple nominal liabilities»[1].

---

[1] *Nersesov N.O.* Aforementioned work. P. 163–165.

Proof of the inevitability
of mistakes in legislation

The theory of mistakes is the branch of mathematic statistics upon the basis of which the methodology of the exposure and evaluation of errors (mistakes) developed. As a completely developed, strong mathematic apparatus, it has inter-disciplinary significance and may be applied to any conceptual apparatus and in any field: in physics, chemistry, biology, sociology, history and also in law.

In the theory of complex systems it is proved that any complex system (a system consisting of a large number of complex, interlinking elements with complex and diverse links) will definitely contain one or more mistakes. In addition, knowing the approximate complexity of the system and probability of mistakes, it is possible to calculate their number with sufficient precision.

This rule is used particularly often in information technology and its branch, i.e. programming, where it is well-known that any complex program will necessarily contain a mistake(s). An example of this could be the *Windows* 95 program, which, despite being issued by the huge corporation *Microsoft,* still contains a large number of errors, which can be discovered by almost any competent user. The presence of mistakes in this program is normal, as the capacity of the hard disk is 80 MB, which is equal to 640,000,000,000 elementary bytes.

Some of the indicators of a complex system are the complexity of the conceptual apparatus and the complexity of relationships between concepts. For example, in the binary code there are two concepts in total: zero and one. There are also two relationships: addition and negation. At the same time, in mathematical analysis, the concept of the variable is even harder to define, and so is the complex relations of the integral and factorial. In legislation the notions themselves are rather complex (for example, gangsterism or contraband), and the same can be said of the logical relations of inclusion, exclusion, complex equality etc. It is therefore necessary to note the immensely large number of concepts, used in law and the very large number of different types of interlinks between the most varied norms, both within laws as well as between them. Consequently it is possible to state with confidence that from the point of view of mathematical statistics law is a complex system.

Thus, knowing that:

*   legislation is a complex system,
*   a complex system necessarily contains mistakes,

we can conclude that **legislation necessarily contains mistakes and the more complex and ramified the law, the more mistakes will be contained within it.**

It thus follows that in many laws high in content and complexity, the presence of mistakes is highly probable.

Following on from the theory of complex systems, it is possible to reveal the following norm:

$N \sim C,$

Where N is the number of mistakes; C is the cybernetic (information) complexity of the norm.

Accordingly, complexity is directly proportional to:

1) the volume of the norm (V);
2) the number of legal links between concepts (LC):

$C \sim V \times LC.$

It is also well-known that the more «worn in» the law, the more thought through, the more times it has been examined and debated, then the less mistakes it will contain, i.e.

$N \sim 1/NE,$

where NE is the number of examinations.

Equally the application of the law affects its «worn-in-ness». It is obvious that the law on theft, applied by courts quite often, is better thought through than, for example, the law on changes of citizenship, which is applied extremely rarely.

$N \sim 1/NA,$

Where NA is the number of applications.

Then we get the formula:

$N \sim V \times LC/NA \times NE.$

From this formula it is possible to conclude that there are more mistakes in laws which:

1) are complex in their wording;
2) are strongly interlinked;
3) are passed in haste;

4) are formulated without considering the positive experience of foreign legislators;

5) are borrowed from legislation of another country, but with an inaccurate translation;

6) have not been applied before i.e. are being applied for the first time.

The chapters of the Civil Code of the Russian Federation which deal with money, securities, banking operations and entrusted administration can be described using all of the above-listed properties.

And although we are obliged to observe laws (even if they contain mistakes), it should not follow that they are regarded as a dogma. It is necessary to facilitate the removal of contradictions in the legislation when they are revealed.

Why there are many mistakes in continental (including Russian) legislation

Economic theory teaches us that the role of the basis is primary, and the role of the superstructure secondary. Transferring this teaching to the field of civil law, one can confirm that industrial strengths and industrial relations (basis) form the standard behaviour of a subject in society, but the government, recognising this said norm, translates it into a legal statute (superstructure).

With the development of industrial relations (basis), old norms of behaviour are dying out and changing shape, new ones are arising, which creates preconditions for the timely correction of legal superstructure — legislation.

Such correcting is carried out much more simply in Anglo-American law, than in continental law (including Russian law).

In the Anglo-American system it is recognised that at the beginning a norm is formed by life itself, and then regulated by law. The principle «Norm is primary, law is secondary» is realised by the principle «the law of justice is higher than general law».

In Russia, like in the rest of continental Europe, German normative theory has been put into practice using the principle «law above all». When this happened, nobody seemed to notice that the legal superstructure (legislation) sometimes does not relate to the altered basis and sometimes laws simply impede the development of normal economic relations.

In the USA and Great Britain, a correct and timely decision on a concrete case may be made by courts, based on the principle «the law of justice is higher than general law». In Russia, however, a long procedure is necessary in order to change or make an addition to a law, which subjectively guarantees that mistakes in legislation have a longer «shelf-life».

As long as economic relations in Russia depend on a legal standard and not the other way round, we are doomed to be lead by legislation which contains a large number of mistakes, wasting our strengths not on fruitful activity, but on surmounting barriers standing in the way of market relations.

Bibliography

1. *Agarkov M.M. A* study of securities. Moscow, 1993.
2. *R. Barr.* Political economy. In 2 vol. Vol. 2. Moscow, 1995.
3. *Bartošek M.* Roman law (notions, terms, definitions): Translated from Czech. Moscow, 1989.
4. *Baskakova M.A.* Businessman's Juridical Dictionary. Moscow, 1994.
5. *Byelov V.A.* On currency convertibility // *Business and banks*, 1996. Issue 26.
6. *Byelov V.A.* Securities in Russian civil right. Moscow, 1996.
7. *Berger. P.* The money mechanism. Moscow, 1993.
8. *Berezina. M. P.* Credit money: an academic essay for practical use // *Business and banks.* 2003. Issue 21–22.
9. *Buslenko N.P., Kalashnikov V.V., Kovalenko I.N.* Lectures on the theory of complex systems. Moscow, 1973.
10. *Woelfel C. J.* Encyclopedia of banking affairs and finances. Samara, 2000.
11. *Gaius.* Institutes. Books 1–4. Moscow, 1997.
12. *Gates B.* The road into the future. Moscow, 1997.
13. German law. Part 1: German Civil Code. Moscow, 1996.
14. *Gryaznova A. G.* Finance and credit encyclopaedic dictionary. Moscow, 2002.
15. Economic theory digest: textbook / Edited by V.M. Sokolinsky. Moscow, 1998.
16. Digests of Justinian. Selected excerpts. Moscow: Nauka, 1984.
17. *Efimova L.G.* Is tax payment by «dead» money a possibility? // *Business and banks*, 1998. Issue 42.
18. *Kapelyushnikov R. I.* Economic theory of property law (methodology, basic concepts, circle of problems). Moscow, 1991.
19. *Katz L.Z., Malyshev V.P.,* Russian Paper Monetary Units Encyclopedia, Vol. 1. Saint-Petersburg, 1998.
20. *Kashin Yu. I.* On the subject of modifying the functions of money // *Money and credit*, 2002. Issue. 1.
21. *Kirillov V.I., Starchenko A.A.* Logic. Moscow, 1995.
22. Currency and credit under capitalism. / Edited by L. N. Krasavina. Moscow, 1980.
23. International currency, credit and financial relations / Edited by L.N. Krasavina. Moscow, 2000.
24. *Cribb. J.* Money. Dorling Kindersley, 1999.

25. *Krivtsov V.D.* Averse: Catalogue for Collectors. M. 1999
26. Course of economic theory / Edited by Chepurin M.N., Kiselyova E.A. Kirov, 1997.
27. *Lazarev V.V.* Gaps in legislation and ways of removing them. Moscow, 1974.
28. *Lavrushin O. I.* Money, credit, banks. Moscow, 1999.
29. *London J.* The Feathers of the Sun. Moscow, 1999.
30. *McConnell C. R., Brue S. L.* Economics: principles, problems and politics. Moscow, 1992.
31. *Maltsev Yu., Shkarinov I.* On the problem of guarantee-free indisputable money withdrawing from banks' correspondent accounts // *Business and banks*, 1996. Issues 22–23.
32. *Mankiw N. G.* The principles of economics. St. Petersburg, 1999.
33. *Marx K.* Capital. A critique of political economy. Vol. I // K. Marx, F. Engels. Complete works.Vol. 23. Moscow, 1960.
34. *Marchenko M.N.* General theory of the State and law. Moscow, 1998.
35. *Melnikova A. S.* The money of Russia. 1000 years. Moscow, 2000.
36. Microeconomics. Theory and Russian practice: textbook for higher education students / Edited by A.G. Gryaznova and A.Yu. Yudanov. Moscow, 1999.
37. *Mikhaelis A. E., Kharlamov L. A.* Russian paper money. Perm, 1993.
38. *Miller R.L., Van Hoose D.D.,* Modern money and banking. Moscow, 2000.
39. *Murzin D. V.* Securities are incorporeal entities. Legal problems with the modern theory of securities. Moscow, 1998.
40. *Nersesov N. O.* Representation and securities in civil law. Moscow, 1998.
41. *Nersesyants V.S.* A History of Political and Legal Studies. Moscow, 1998.
42. *Nersesyants V.S.* Philosophy of law. Moscow, 1998.
43. *Novitsky I.B., Peretersky I.S.* Roman private law. Moscow, 1996
44. *North D.* Institutes, institutional changes and functioning of the economy. Moscow, 1997.
45. General economic theory. Political economy / Edited by V.I. Vidiapin, G.P. Zhuravlyova. Moscow, 1995.
46. *Orlenko L.V.* The history of trade. Moscow, 2006.
47. The complete Laws of the Russian Empire. Vol. 15. Code: E 121/1; H, 19/3158.

48. *Polterovich V. M.* On the road to a new reform theory // *Economic studies of modern Russia*, 1999. Issue 3.
49. *Portnoy M. A.* Money, its forms and functions. Moscow, 1998.
50. *Posner R. A.* Economic analysis of law. Moscow, 2005.
51. Russian Legal Encyclopaedia. Moscow, 1999.
52. *Reisberg B. A., Lozovskii L. S., Starodubtseva E. B.* Modern Economic Dictionary. Moscow: INFRA-M, 2006.
53. *Savatier R.* Theory of obligations. Moscow, 1972
54. *Sadikov O.N.* Commentary on the Civil Code of the RF, Part I. Moscow, 1995.
55. *Sklovsky K. I.* Ownership in civil law. Moscow, 1999
56. *Sokolinsky V.M.* The State and economics: textbook. Moscow, 1997.
57. *Sukhanov E. A.* Objects of property law // *Law*, 1995. Issue 4.
58. *Sukhanov E. A.* Civil Law. Vol. 1. Moscow, 1998.
59. *Shershenevich G. F.* Manual of Russian civil law. Moscow, 1995.
60. Economics: textbook of «economic theory» course / Edited by A.S. Bulatov. Moscow, 1997.
61. Economic theory: textbook for higher education students / Edited by V.D. Kamayev. Moscow, 1998.
62. Economic theory (Political economy): textbook. Edited by A.G. Gryaznova, T.V. Checheleva. Moscow, 1997.
63. Economic theory of national economics and global economy (Political economy): textbook. Edited by A.G. Gryaznova, T.V. Checheleva. Moscow, 1997.
64. *Enneccerus L.* Course of German Civil Law. Moscow, 1950.
65. Encyclopedia of banking and finance/ Edited by C. J. Woelfel. Samara, 2000.
66. *F. A. Hayek.* Private money. Tver, 1996.
67. *L. Harris.* Monetary theory. Moscow: Progress, 1990.
68. *Hicks J.R.* Value and Capital. Moscow: Progress, 1993.
69. *S. B. Tsereteli* On the system of logical development of idea forms // *Voprosy philosophii*, 1967. Issue 2.
70. Encyclopaedia Americana. Vol. 19. 1988.
71. Clifford Chance Moscow office. «An overview of euro-obligations issue» March 1997.
72. *Pick Albert, Colin R. Bruce II, Neil Shafer.* Standard catalogue of world paper money. Iola WI, 1960.
73. http://www.i-a-m.ws/
74. http://www.inline.ru/

Contents

Part IV. MISTAKES IN LEGISLATION AND THE ROLE OF ECONOMIC THEORY

www.ingramcontent.com/pod-product-compliance
Lightning Source LLC
Chambersburg PA
CBHW061308220326

41599CB00026B/4792